MENTORSHIFT

DR. WILLIAM H. CURTIS

MentorShift

Dr. William H. Curtis

The Church Online, LLC

1000 Ardmore Blvd.

Pittsburgh, PA 15221

International Standard Book Number:

978-1-940786-70-4

Library of Congress Catalogue Number: Available Upon Request

Scripture quotations are from the ESV® Bible (The Holy Bible, English Standard Version®), copyright © 2001 by Crossway, a publishing ministry of Good News Publishers. Used by permission. All rights reserved.

Scripture quotations marked NASB taken from the NEW AMERICAN STANDARD BIBLE®, Copyright © 1960, 1962, 1963, 1968, 1971, 1972, 1973, 1975, 1977, 1995 by The Lockman Foundation. Used by permission.

Scripture quotations marked (NIV) are taken from the Holy Bible, New International Version®, NIV®. Copyright © 1973, 1978, 1984, 2011 by Biblica, Inc.™ Used by permission of Zondervan. All rights reserved worldwide. www.zondervan.com The "NIV" and "New International Version" are trademarks registered in the United States Patent and Trademark Office by Biblica, Inc.™

Printed in the United States of America

Published by The Church Online, LLC

TABLE OF CONTENTS

INTRODUCTION
What is God's Role for Christians Today?

The world has changed more in the last fifty years than in the previous two hundred. We have gone from black and white televisions to 4k Netflix on our cellphones. Technology isn't the only way that the world has changed, either. Today, people have taken to advances in medical science to change their bodies, alter their minds, and have even begun to modify the DNA of children.

However, in many ways the world has also stayed the same. In our world, hatred and bigotry still exist and racial and ethnic relations are as tense as ever. Pollution and environmental destruction continue, and even the question of sexual identity is as old as humanity itself. But now, questions on these topics have been brought to the forefront of the mind of the church.

As Christians, we must be prepared to truly lead in this new world. In spite of the climate of the times, we know that God is unchanging, and we can look to His Word for solutions. As Titus 1:9 says, "He must hold firm to the trustworthy word as taught so that he may be able to give instruction from sound doctrine and also to rebuke those who contradict it."[1]

---

[1] Titus 1:9

7

During this era, we are called by God to be ethical mentors in the lives of those around us, whether we are pastors, church leaders, or laypeople in the church. Our assignment is a holy one and a necessary one, and we are to deny ungodliness and worldly desires, we are to teach about Christ and His mission with all authority, and we should let no one disregard us.[2]

We have a divine mandate to help others navigate the chaos of this new world with Christ as our touchstone. Christ is "the image of the invisible God, the firstborn of all creation," and "He is before all things and in Him all things hold together."[3] Only with His power can we help to guide our people through this world. However, we can't expect to simply receive Christ's guidance and be fully equipped. To eat, we must work.[4]

To raise up our family in Christ in this day and age, we must put in the time to understand and anticipate the issues and questions that will arise. We do not live in a time where we can expect people to listen to us unquestioningly, and that is a good thing. But that means we cannot fall asleep to the needs of those around us.[5]

To protect ourselves and our brothers and sisters in Christ from flighty and ephemeral pop-philosophies

---

[2]   Titus 2:11-15

[3]   Colossians 1:15-17

[4]   2 Thessalonians 3:10

[5]   1 Thessalonians 5:6

and fads,[6] we must be well educated and prepared. Just like praying before a test won't guarantee an A, we cannot expect to succeed against the enemy if we are isolated and insular. We must study.

With careful study of God's Word and a divinely affected study of the world we live in, we will be equipped to be the ethical mentors that God requires.

Only by taking these steps and understanding the world that we live in can we hope to be effective mentors. It is important that we keep Christ before us as a guide and that we guide those that we mentor to become followers of Christ above all.

---

[6]   Ephesians 4:11-16

CHAPTER 1
Burning Questions

When Moses encountered God at the burning bush, he asks God two questions: "Who am I?" and "Who should I tell them sent me?"[1] Deep in those questions is also a third, "Why should they listen?"

Moses was encountering a long-silent God, and he was a long-exiled prince. Moses was no one to the Israelites and no one to the Egyptians. Today, many of us feel similarly. We are a lost voice in the cacophony of the modern world. We may even find that our connection to God has long since dried up. However, God makes the same demands of us that He made of Moses, and we see these demands reflected in the Great Commission.

We are not alone in these questions. Our modern world asks the same questions, and God alone can provide the answers to them.

Moses did not understand who God was when he faced Him at the burning bush, but over time, Moses went from the burning bush to God's true revelation on Sinai.[2] God did not instantaneously transform Moses but walked with him from the lonely encounter at the burning bush for many years until He revealed Himself to Moses.

Like Moses, our calling involves walking with God so that we can properly help and mentor those around us. Moses returned to the people of Israel with the name of a long-forgotten God, and the results of his efforts were bleak. The Israelites continued to fail and

---

[1]   Exodus 3

[2]   Exodus 33:18-23

falter, just like we continue to do today. In ourselves, we have no panacea for sinfulness, and our role as Christians is not to save the world. Christ is the only solution, but we have a responsibility to communicate who Christ is to this world that doesn't know His name.

While many of us live in countries where Christ is a common name, we would be myopic to suggest that the majority of those around us understand Christ in a meaningful way. Burdened with stereotypes and misinformation, many who call themselves Christians show none of the transformation that we would expect from someone who is a follower of Christ. Even more, those outside the Church often view Christ as nothing more than a slur and God as nothing more than a malevolent judge—if they believe He exists at all.

As Christians, we have had our burning bush encounter, but many of the people we meet every day have never had one or forgotten theirs. Our responsibility is to act like a guide, as Moses did. We may not be the best speaker or most intelligent, but we have been chosen by God and have a role to play in the lives of our neighbors.

We must take this responsibility seriously and continue to walk towards our Mt. Sinai while bringing our Israelites, our friends, family, and neighbors, with us.

These questions, "Who am I?" "Who should I tell them sent me?" and "Why should they listen?" require answers. Without the answers to these questions, Moses would have never been able to help free the Israelites.

God answers Moses' question "Who am I?" without regard to Moses. When God asserts, "Certainly I will be with you, and this shall be the sign to you that it is I who have sent you. When you have brought the people out of Egypt, you shall worship God at this mountain,"[3] He is telling Moses that his identity is embedded in a promise and in God's relationship to Moses.

God assures Moses that he is worthy of delivering God's message, not because of who he is but because of who he will become. God is looking beyond Moses' temporal scope and is speaking to the future Moses—the greatest of all prophets.[4] God speaks to our question "Who am I?" by telling us that we will become his sons and daughters, little Christs.[5]

Without participating in this transformation, we have no hope to affect those around us. Moses was successful because he approached God with due reverence. He was bold, but he understood that God was greater than he was. Despite his questions, Moses stepped forward and went to Pharaoh. This was in spite of his status as a criminal and in spite of his distant relationship with his fellow Israelites.

Similarly, we must step out into our calling, and our calling is not an esoteric, ephemeral mystery to be divined. It is simple: to love God with all your heart,

---

[3]   Exodus 3:12 NASB

[4]   Deuteronomy 34:10

[5]   2 Corinthians 6:18; *Mere Christianity,* C.S. Lewis

mind, and soul and to love your neighbor as yourself.[6] What we do for a job or where we go in our free time is secondary to how we love God and love our neighbors. Only when we operate in love of God and neighbor can we begin to understand who we are. Only when we understand who we are can we then begin to mentor those around us.

Moses exemplifies this. Due to his love for God and his neighbor, his people who he was never a part of, he chose to leave his life and take on a new one—one that he did not want. Moses grew dramatically over this time guiding the Israelites, and he only became a great, unquestioned leader towards the end of his life. When he first led the Israelites out of Egypt, many of them wanted to abandon him and turn back.[7]

Similarly, we must persevere and grow throughout our lives, so that we can maintain our relationships with those around us and so that we can maintain our relationship with God. Without these two key relationships in place, we will find that those we try to mentor turn their backs on us when we lead them to the Red Sea.

Moses' question, "Who should I tell them sent me?" receives a more mystical answer than the first. God responds, "I AM WHO I AM."[8] This declaration rejects understanding. God delivers to Moses the tetragrammaton, the formal name of God, and asserts

---

6   Matthew 22:37-40

7   Exodus 14:11

8   Exodus 3:14

that He is not fit for descriptors. He rejects that He could be understood but concedes to Moses. He understands that Moses cannot come to the Israelites and declare that I AM WHO I AM sent him. But instead, God shows Moses how to reveal a facet of who God is to them—a facet fit for the hearer. God reminds Moses and the Israelites of who He is *to* them. He is the God of their fathers, Abraham, Isaac, and Jacob.[9]

Our infinite God, too, speaks to us in ways that are meaningful to us. He is deeply personal and reveals the parts of Him that are the most beneficial for us. The Israelites would not rally around some esoteric deity, but the reminder of their heritage and the promises of their ancestors showed them the truth of God: He is their deliverer.

For our modern world, a deliverer is exactly what we need. Decades beyond the civil rights movement, the condition of the hearts of men has not changed. Even still, ethnic and race-based hatred is alive around the world, from American racism to persecuted tribes and peoples, and there are also those who many in the church persecute and hate for their sexual or gender orientation, namely those who belong to the LGBT[10] community.

No matter what one believes about any of these topics, it is indisputably true that all of mankind is in need of

---

[9]   Exodus 3:15

[10]   LGBT, or Lesbian, Gay, Bisexual, and Transgender, is shorthand for any of those who find themselves affiliated with that community and is not limited to those specific terms.

a deliverer. Today, God's message rings true. He is the God of Abraham, Isaac, and Jacob, and we have all received a measure of grace to be welcomed into that family.[11] We are the chosen people of God, and our goal is to bring Christ to the world.

And lastly, we arrive at the deep question hidden in the text: "Why should they listen?" Of all the questions Moses had, this one is the most poignant. Here, Moses is the shunned, Egyptian-adopted Israelite. He belongs to no one and to nothing, but God declared to him that the future Moses was worthy.

God's answer to "Why should they listen?" is independent of Moses and is independent of us. They should listen because God is truth. As we walk in our faith and become more like Christ, we reduce ourselves and more of God's truth consumes us.[12] So, the answer to the question is as powerful as God Himself. They should listen because God is the source of life, and He wants us to have it abundantly.[13]

When we come to a mature place and understand this, we can be agents of healing and reconciliation to those around us. We can properly mentor and advise those who are in need. This is precisely because we have taken the steps to minimize ourselves and to raise up God in our lives.

---

[11]   Romans 11:17

[12]   John 3:30, Hebrews 12:29

[13]   John 10:10

As we embark on this journey to become ethical mentors for those in our lives, whether we are bishops, pastors, deacons, or laypeople, we must be grounded in God. We must continue to profess the truth that God has revealed to us and continue to journey towards Mt. Sinai, full of expectation and hope that along the way God will transform us.

CHAPTER 2
'm not Religious.
'm Spiritual.

Our world is pressured by expansive, technological advancement. More than ever before, humanity has gone from fighting to survive to thriving. Our post World War II world has greeted us with unprecedented peace and prosperity, but within that, people have dismissed God. Within a few decades, many people have moved into a new type of faith: spiritual pluralism.

You may have heard or even used, the phrase "I'm not religious. I'm spiritual." Sometimes, this is a way for people to distance themselves from corrupt members of a church. Other times, this also means that people have chosen to practice their Christianity in a way that's unique to them.

While Christianity is inherently pluralistic, being as everyone practices their faith in their own, personal way, most Christians believe that there are a set of core beliefs that are required for people to call themselves "Christians." In this vein, many Christians reject groups such as Mormons and Jehovah's Witnesses as "Christian" because they don't share core beliefs that have existed in Christianity since its beginning.

When our spirituality becomes purely pluralistic, however, it becomes uprooted. If people believe that they can choose for themselves between what is right or wrong, they are ignoring one of the foundational parts of Christianity, that Christ is the truth.[1] By taking it upon themselves to re-imagine or disagree with the normative principles in Christ's teachings, they step into the murky realms of spiritual pluralism.

---

[1]   John 14:6

WHO AM I?

Spiritual pluralism is the idea that one can create and mold the truth to fit themselves. A spiritual pluralist believes that simply being a good person is enough for salvation. No longer is the Bible, church, or pastor a key authority in the lives of churchgoers. Each person has become their own authority.

Spiritual pluralism has taken to Moses' question with fervor. "Who am I?" drives people to explore themselves and to take the bits of what they enjoy and build their identity up around that. However, a person's individuality is lost in this person-building venture. Afterwards, a person is no longer a person, but an amalgamation of labels and orientations. Individuality is lost in the plurality of labels and values that a person defines themselves by.

Similarly, churchgoers have a strong desire to find purpose in their lives. Many churchgoers delve deep into what they believe God's plan is for their lives. Often times these people hold onto the misguided belief that God wants them to take a specific job or move to a certain city because, deep down, they are looking for approval from God to do what they already want to do. This is dangerous, pluralistic Christianity: choosing to accept our thoughts and ideas as from God based solely on the notion that we like them or feel like they define our identities well or will gain us recognition as being "spiritual."

The key issue that our modern world and spiritual pluralism raises is identity. Many of the people in our lives are simply choosing who they want to be in the moment and defending themselves against any critique or criticism. Instead of being Joe or Mary, they are an artist or a Republican, burying themselves within their chosen label and trying to live up to an idealized reality.

As ethical mentors, it is our job to cut through that shell and expose those around us to the objective and real truth of Christ. We cannot let the desire for personal happiness in ourselves or our family and friends override the value and necessity of the truth of God's Word. If we can learn anything from Christ's life, it is that the road is hard, but the reward is great.[2]

THE FAILURE OF THE CHURCH

The church is not the pillar of society that it once was, and today everyone's faith is so personal that it has become mutable. From 2007 to 2014, the "religious none," those who describe themselves as religious but have no affiliation to a church, has grown by seven percent.[3] And it is only going to keep growing.

Spiritual pluralism does not search for objective truth but exchanges it for personal truth. When applied to faith, we find that this idea undermines the veracity and value of the Christian faith altogether. Looking for

---

[2]   Matthew 10

[3]   *Why people with no religion are projected to decline as a share of the world's population,* Pew Research Center, 2017

"Looking for cheap and easy gratification, the current world hopes to simply satiate themselves rather than dig deep into uncomfortable truths, even if that means abandoning the church."

---

cheap and easy gratification, the current world hopes to simply satiate themselves rather than dig deep into uncomfortable truths, even if that means abandoning the church.

Moses was no stranger to this pain. When he asked God, "Who am I that I should go to Pharaoh and bring the children of Israel out of Egypt?" Moses had carved out a new life away from his past pain of Egypt and the moral dilemma that he had left behind. He knew full well, having killed an Egyptian, he was a traitor and a criminal.

Having killed the truth, many of those around us will balk at the idea of proselytizing. They will reject the notion of Christianity being the true way. Instead they will suggest that Christ is not the only way to the Father, and they will advocate that being a good person is enough to enter heaven.

Our world of spiritual pluralism has reduced our effectiveness as mentors, teachers, and preachers of the Gospel. More and more, the church is regarded as a think tank for moral value, with one person's perspective weighed equally with anyone else's. The Bible and the Gospel are no longer the source of truth, and the preacher is no longer viewed as a guide through the Bible.

The question "Who am I?" necessarily tears down the individual. It is a failure to recognize the already-but-not-yet reality that we are children of God. However, the church has failed to deliver this message. Because of this failure, we have allowed our fellow Christians to go out into different, dangerous pastures.

Now, we find ourselves rescuing our friends and family, pulling them out of the muddled belief that the world is theirs to define. The desire to have control and power has led to our present pluralism. Instead of conforming to His image,[4] we have taken to conforming God to our image.

The life of the Christian is one of self-sacrifice, and this flies in the face of the world's current pluralistic tendencies. The Christian is forced to bend the knee to Christ and to say, "Not my will but yours."[5] Only from that place can we plant seeds into those we mentor. If we believe that we can mentor and guide those who have no desire to be mentored, we are fooling ourselves.

---

[4]   Romans 8:29

[5]   Luke 22:42

WHO SHOULD I TELL THEM SENT ME?

In the face of pluralism, we have to fight to establish a true ontology, or understanding of our world. We must diffuse the dangerous idea that anyone can define their own faith for themselves. Instead, our obligation to those around us is to understand the true faith ourselves.

Part of this is to understand who sent us. When we ask God, "Who should I tell them sent me?" we find that the best answer for the spiritual pluralist is the answer that God gives Moses. God declares that I AM WHO I AM. He does not give Moses that answer to confuse him, but to rather reveal something about His own being.

The idea that God 'is who He is' is a profound and powerful concept. God is telling Moses here that God is a self-contained, self-sufficient God. He is also telling Moses that all the stories about God's person that have been passed down from Abraham, Isaac, and Jacob are a reflection of God.

God's essential being can only be summed up by saying that God equals God. But we can also take this a step further. God is also telling Moses that God is who He says that He is. So, when we look forward to Christ, the incarnate God, we see that when Christ argues that He is "the way, the truth, and the life,"[6] He is showing us something true about Himself. He is

---

[6]   John 14:6

truth. All true things refer to God and find their truth in Him. So, in today's world where truth is a cheap word, we can reinforce ourselves by embodying Christ and exemplifying real truth.

When we can embody the truth of Christ, we can draw the people in our lives into life with Christ. We can help to pull them out of the depression and anxiety that their pluralistic worldview has buried them in.

We live in a world that has seen vast increases in mental health challenges, and the church has an answer to those problems. There is no cure-all on this side of eternity, but the joy of the Lord can and should be present in the lives of Christians. The compassion and love of the church is a necessity for our broken, selfish world.

WHY SHOULD THEY LISTEN?

Many times, the hard work begins from within. To understand why others should listen to us, we must first understand who we are and work on ourselves.

While we will continue to be sinful people, we cannot hope to be ethical mentors if we are not ourselves firmly grounded. The blind cannot lead the blind.[7] We must work out our salvation with fear and trembling,[8]

---

[7]   Matthew 15:14

[8]   Philippians 2:12

"Our primary goal as ethical mentors is to illuminate the truth. More than anything, we are lights that reflect God."

and from that place of devotion to God, we can pour out His life into others.

Moses was correct when he questioned, "Who am I?" He *was* a murderer. He *was* a sinner. We are, too. However, we can't just walk away from God's calling because we aren't yet perfect. Instead, we walk into His calling precisely due to that imperfection. Through our role as ethical mentors, God will transform and shape us into holy people.

Just like Moses, we must go to the Pharaohs of our lives and show them God's truth.

Our primary goal as ethical mentors is to illuminate the truth. More than anything, we are lights that reflect God. Paul put it succinctly when he wrote the words, "But we all, with unveiled face, beholding as in a mirror the glory of the Lord, are being transformed into the same image from glory to glory."[9] As we reflect Christ to others, we become transformed to be like Him.

As we reflect Christ's glory into the lives of others, we expose them to the truth. However, we cannot

---

[9]   2 Corinthians 3:18 NASB

expect everyone to be convinced. For Moses, Pharaoh did not convert. Pharaoh's change of heart was short-lived. However, we must persevere, because if Moses had faltered when Pharaoh changed his mind, the Israelites would have died.

So, as we begin to mentor, we cannot let ourselves become overwhelmed by perceived failures. The transformative power is not us, but it is the reflected glory of God.[10] Instead, our goal is to do our best to bring Christ into our world and to show Him to those around us. Only then can we hope to build the relationships that will shape the world for generations ahead of us.

---

[10]   2 Corinthians 3:18

CHAPTER 3
It's More than Creation Versus Evolution

Alongside and distinct from spiritual pluralism, another worldview has come to prominence in the past half-century. Instead of reshaping the spiritual, *scientism* views the world entirely through the lens of science.

Science is good and beneficial. Without it we would go back to the age of rampant disease and infant mortality. Science has helped us to understand the world and to create a world that has brought about more prosperity, understanding, and healing than ever before. With all of that said, scientism takes science too far.

Too far, in this case, means that scientism believes that everything can be understood through the lens of science. It reduces everything to a science experiment, even concepts like love and truth. When science is applied to ideas that science had never explored before, some alarming conclusions come to light.

When love is reduced to a chemical reaction in the brain, the real experience of a married couple is demystified and, in many cases, ruined. When the experience of humanity is brought down to nothing more than chemicals, it opens up ethics to the whims of the individual. Concepts like right and wrong fall away, because science cannot give us answers to those things. So many adherents of scientism suggest that right and wrong are made up, and that means they don't view things like murder, slavery, or governmental corruption as inherently wrong.

The issue of scientism is not the creation and evolution debate. There are many Christians who believe in

---

"God called Moses because of who Moses would become, not because of who Moses was."

---

evolution and many who don't. The issue of scientism is that it logically concludes that some of the darkest parts of humanity are not truly wrong.

WHO AM I?

In this worldview, scientism is a reductionist approach to how we acquire knowledge. It takes all of the emotions and experiences that humans have and reduces them down to chemical reactions. Ultimately, scientism comes to the same conclusion as spiritual pluralism: anything goes. However, scientism takes it further and really means it.

Scientism says that the individual is just a series of chemical reactions and is completely changeable with a change of hormones. A person can be made happy or sad just by adjusting how much serotonin they have in their brain. A man can be made into a woman and a woman into a man with a few surgeries and some hormonal adjustments as well. Identity itself is under attack in this worldview. A person could be made beautiful or ugly by editing their genes. One could be remade into whatever they want to be, and no limits should be placed on their desires.

Moses' question, "Who am I?" addresses scientism well. Moses' identity to God was not contingent on Moses. Moses was chosen by God in spite of himself. God shows us that our identity is not rooted in the chemical reactions in our body, but in God Himself. God called Moses because of who Moses would become, not because of who Moses was.

Similarly, scientism's answer that humans are just chemicals cannot stand up to the experiential reality that humanity does experience love and knows right or wrong. Anyone who has had children knows that, even without being taught, children know when they've done something wrong.[1]

As Christians and ethical mentors, part of the gravity of the burgeoning philosophy of scientism is how destructive it is to peoples' sense of self and self-worth. By leaning into our knowledge that mankind is fearfully and wonderfully made[2] by God, we can bring to light the intrinsic value of human beings.

It is important for us to communicate how valuable humanity is to God, and we can highlight that with the experiential reality of every person. We want nothing more than to be successful and healthy. Even the most severely depressed or suicidal individual wants nothing more than to be healthy and whole. A sick man who begs to die doesn't want to die, but he wants to be full of life.

---

[1] *Research Shows toddlers understand right from wrong at just 19 months,* Association for Psychological Science, 2012

[2] Psalm 139:14

"A selfless, authentic faith does more than any amount of apologetics or arguing. Many times, people are converted to a philosophy or religion not because of logic, but because of experiences."

When it comes to scientism, Christianity replaces mere chemicals with fullness and meaning. Humanity is a recipient of Christ's life. When we live a life that is an example of this, we act as an antithesis to the ideas that scientism presents. We prove through our living that we are valuable and that others are valuable.

WHO SHOULD I TELL THEM SENT ME?

Scientism is a greater challenge to Christianity than spiritual pluralism. A spiritual pluralist acquiesces to the spiritual, but a proponent of scientism rejects it outright. Simply suggesting that God exists is not going to cut it for these people.

Instead, long-term sustained relationships will be the only thing that can affect change in the lives of those who engage in scientism. A selfless, authentic faith does more than any amount of apologetics or arguing.

Many times, people are converted to a philosophy or religion not because of logic, but because of experiences. Those who adhere to scientism are likely to have been hurt by Christians or Christianity, so they find comfort in scientism because it attempts to tear down Christianity as prattling self-help.

The current generation of young adults, Millennials, are more likely to be unaffiliated with religion.[3] For the past several generations in America, we've seen nothing but decline in church attendance. So, it is our responsibility to share Christianity with them. Part of that is to convey who Christ is to them. While many people have learned about Christ, many more have almost no understanding of His Gospel.

Outside of Christianity, many people have reduced Christ to a good moral teacher at best. Many more have no idea that Christ's mission was to come to the earth and save mankind from their sins. In the same vein, the Gospel has been reduced to: be kind, and you will be saved. Knowing all this, it is imperative that we present the Gospel with love and relationship.

When it comes to Moses' question, we should tell them that the God of love sent us, but not with our words, but our actions. Only then can those around us be truly convinced by the powerful work of Christ in our lives.

---

[3] *Religion Among the Millennials,* Pew Research Center, 2010

"Only in the confines of genuine relationship, not fruitless debate, can we hope to draw those with a bleak outlook on life to the full life that Christ provides."

WHY SHOULD THEY LISTEN?

Christianity brings hope to a dying world. Without Christ, humanity is doomed to destruction. Even in an atheistic worldview, humanity is bound for destruction and emptiness. Christianity, instead, provides a hope and a future for mankind.

When we bring fullness of life to our relationships, scientism comes face to face with possibility. This possibility and hope can overcome and eclipse the pessimism that scientism carries. A lived out, personal Christianity is the only hope for bringing healing to this deep-seated pessimism.

Any individual who comes in contact with true Christianity will have to acknowledge it, and living our lives as Christians is how we can bring wholeness to the world around us. More than debates or facts, personal relationships demand attention. Only in the confines of genuine relationship, not fruitless debate, can we hope to draw those with a bleak outlook on life to the full life that Christ provides.

This requires us to participate in our faith. Christianity does not bring about salvation by works, but salvation certainly produces them. Only by truly expressing our Christianity is it beneficial to others. Again, this reminds us of the work we must personally do to become effective ethical mentors. We cannot expect to help anyone if we are drowning. So, by participating in the fullness of life that Christ gives us, we can inspire those around us to where we are.

We can choose to disengage from fruitless debates, and we can choose to engage the individual. We can help our brothers and sisters when they are ill. We can give of ourselves even when it is not convenient.

To truly combat the pessimism of scientism, we need not look any further than Christ's summation of the law: "You shall love the Lord your God with all your heart and with all your soul and with all your strength and with all your mind, and your neighbor as yourself." [4] Only then can we bring healing to those around us and guide them towards the Truth.

---

[4]   Luke 10:27 ESV

CHAPTER 4
Ethical Mentoring in the Modern World

In 2018, for the first time that we know of, a scientist has edited a human embryo and that human embryo was brought to term by a mother. These two twin girls, "Lulu" and "Nana," are the very first, living, genetically edited human beings. Using the gene-editing tool CRISPR/Cas9, a team of scientists in China entered territory that had hitherto been banned.

The twins were edited on the gene CCR5, the gene that HIV uses to infect humans, with the hopes of making them immune to the disease. These children were the only surviving embryos of seven but are allegedly healthy babies.[1]

While the research from this lab has yet to be verified and reviewed and we do not know whether the claims are true, this isn't the first time that scientists have edited human embryos. In 2015, a different Chinese lab edited several embryos that were not to be used in in vitro fertilization.[2] This has cascaded into other labs being opened to do the same thing. In 2016, the UK gave permission for labs to use CRISPR to edit donated human embryos, and in 2018 in Japan, permission was given as well. In 2019, reports arose of a privately funded scientist at Columbia University in New York, editing embryos with CRISPR as well.

With this new, burgeoning technology, there are certainly rewards to be reaped, but there are also

---

[1] *World's first gene-edited babies created in China, claims scientist,* The Guardian, 2018

[2] *Years before CRISPR babies, this man was the first to edit human embryos,* MIT Technology Review, 2018

ethical concerns. A world without HIV is a better world, and a world where genetic diseases can be cured before birth will greatly reduce the suffering of millions, if not billions, of people. However, designer babies, babies edited to have perfect traits, will become commonplace as this technology becomes more and more accessible.

Even more dangerous than editing babies to make them more beautiful or athletic, these changes could result in long-term, unknown genetic consequences for the children of these genetically altered individuals and introduce new, rampant genetic disease into the gene pool. This would be especially true of diseases like Huntington's Disease, which typically appears around the age of thirty, after most people have already had children.

This is not a far distant future but is one that has allegedly already settled upon us. Even if the Chinese lab did not manage to bring an edited embryo to term, it is only a matter of time before some other scientist does. In light of this technology, the church must prepare to be a vocal guide on its ethics.

We must take what we've learned about living a Christian life and use that to our advantage when we speak on these ethical matters. We need to come with an air of relationship and love for humanity. We need to be passionate, but not angry. Only then can we bring about healthy, helpful guidance as we enter this brave new world.

"Thus, we are called to guide mankind, Christian or not, towards what is right and good. Whether they listen is their choice, but we cannot allow ourselves to become complicit in anyone's self-destruction."

WHO AM I?

For many of us today, we may ask the same question Moses did, "Who am I that I should go...?" Few people have PhDs, let alone PhDs in genetics. We may feel unqualified to speak on this topic or to even begin to understand what CRISPR is or what genes even are. For many of us, we learned about genes in school a long time ago, and we know little about how they work.

We may be inclined to just put the issue aside, but this is one of the most dangerous choices that we can make. By deciding that we aren't up to the task, we shirk our responsibility as ethical mentors. We choose to allow others to decide what is right and wrong, instead of injecting what God says is right or wrong into the equation.

When we excuse ourselves, we give up and become complicit. We allow others, who may not be qualified or ready, to make the call on what is right or wrong.

There is nothing in science that allows a scientist to determine right from wrong, but there certainly is something in Christianity that allows us to.

Thus, we are called to guide mankind, Christian or not, towards what is right and good. Whether they listen is their choice, but we cannot allow ourselves to become complicit in anyone's self-destruction. We should never sign off on someone else's sin or misjudgment because we feel lazy or as if it isn't worth our time. We must fight for the benefit of those around us precisely because we love our neighbors.

Christians are also called to be defenders of the weak and of those who cannot defend themselves.[3] By exercising our God-given role as ethical mentors, we can affect the lives of those who others may overlook. When it comes to these specific technological developments, it is important that we defend those, especially embryos, who cannot speak for themselves but are the subject of experimentation.

So, we are called to study and learn as much as we can about the challenges that our world faces. It is our God-given role to prayerfully engage these new ethical dilemmas and become role models and advocates for what is right.

---

[3]   Psalm 82:3

WHO SHOULD I TELL THEM SENT ME?

While Christ tells us not to be ashamed of our faith in Him,[4] claiming that we are correct on any issue simply because we believe in Jesus is equally sinful.[5] If we sling around the name of Christ as an opportunity to win arguments, not only are we insulting Christ but we are not going to win any arguments or hold any sway over people in our lives.

Instead, we should invoke wisdom that is pure, peaceable, gentle, merciful, impartial, and honest.[6] When we gain our wisdom from God and apply that wisdom to study and understanding of new technologies and events, we will be prepared to speak on any subject. We will be ready to engage and listen to different arguments, we will not be quick to judge, and we will respond as informed individuals.

Being willing to engage and listen to those who may have different views than you will allow you to learn from them. You can hear what they have to say about these new and emerging technologies, and you will be able to see any flaws in their logic. When we engage in this type of relational dialogue, criticism is levied with a pure, kind heart and can bring about change.

Few of us are in meetings with important people who make decisions on whether activities like gene editing

---

4   Mark 8:38

5   Exodus 20:7

6   James 3:17

should be legal. However, we do and can influence the court of public opinion. When we help others to arrive at correct, ethical views on emergent technologies, we can help them to correctly influence others. Effectively mentoring those around us will raise them up as ethical mentors for people who we will never meet.

By changing the lives of just a few people, we can set in motion a chain reaction of ethical mentorship. Even if we don't affect the views and feelings of non-Christians, the seed of the Word will take root in them and spread some facet of the truth.

We can only do this when we come to discussions and arguments in the name of wisdom that is fueled by gentleness, understanding, and peacefulness.

WHY SHOULD THEY LISTEN?

Few people understand the extent to which new technology can affect the world. If you watch old cartoons or movies about the future, flying cars abounded by the year 2000, and there was nary a cellphone in sight. However, if you look outside today there are no flying cars at all. The future is impossible to predict, but certainly we ought to be prepared.

If we are not prepared to discuss what might be, we will be unprepared when it arrives. Because we are approaching debates and discussions with a teachable spirit and are willing to spend time studying these emerging technologies, we are as qualified as anyone to prepare others for what might come in the future.

One does not need to have a PhD in genetics to be qualified to have an opinion on whether editing the genes of embryos ought to be legal or not. One can easily understand that these technologies affect humans in ways that are beyond science. A failed experiment on a child brought to term could lead to lifelong suffering for that individual or their children.

When we understand that our concern is not the science itself but the effects of that science on the people around us, we are more than qualified to speak on what is most lifegiving and beneficial for mankind. We, as members of the human race, ought to be listened to precisely because our aim is caring for our neighbors and fellow humans.

By suggesting to others that they preemptively think about these potential futures, we are proving to them that we are qualified by virtue of being concerned and prepared for the future. We show the world that Christians are gearing up to be the vanguard of humanity, protecting it from humanity's own self-destructive tendencies.

That said, we ought not be overly cautious and prohibitive. When we choose to protect children from being the subject of experiments, we also understand that millions of children are born every day with harrowing diseases. CRISPR could save lives and improve more. So, we should not look at the future as a foreboding, dangerous cloud, but we should look at it for what it is: the future of humanity, touched by both mankind's sinfulness and God's grace.

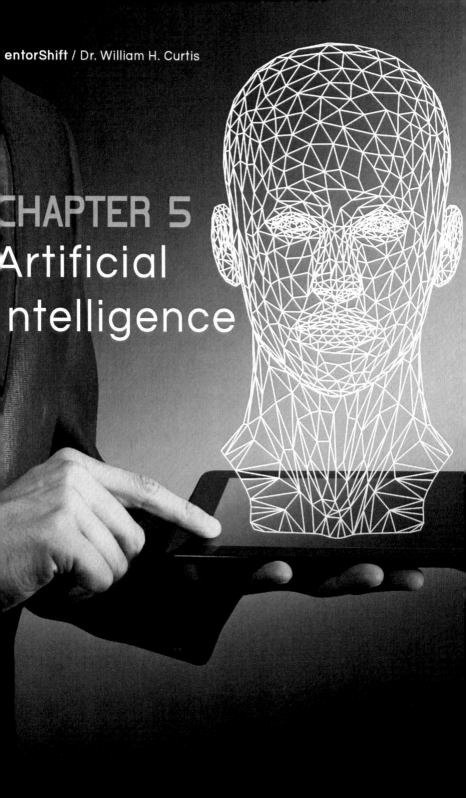

CHAPTER 5
Artificial
ntelligence

In 1994, a computer solved the game of checkers by memorizing every possible move. No longer can a human beat a machine at checkers. While we might think of checkers as a kid's game, Chess met the same fate in 1997.[1]

In 2016, a company called DeepMind created an Artificial Intelligence, or AI, that became the first computer to beat a champion at the board game Go. This computer didn't just memorize all of the moves in Go, as Go is much more complicated than Chess. This AI managed to learn how to think like a Go master. When the first champion lost, most professional Go players thought an AI that would be capable of beating them was at least ten years away.

In December 2018, DeepMind created an AI that was capable of beating pros of the video game *StarCraft II*. The AI, named AlphaStar, managed to beat long-time pro gamer Grzegorz Komincz five games in a row. A video game like *StarCraft II* is an order of magnitude more difficult to compute than Go.

AlphaStar matters, in part, because *StarCraft II* is a war game. Players run the armies of different aliens and try to destroy each other's bases. If we live in a world where some of the best players of a video game can lose to an AI, we need to prepare for a world where AI will be active participants in real wars, and we need to be voices that inform what is right and wrong when it comes to our new technology.

---

[1] *Deepmind beats pros at Starcraft in another triumph for bots,* Wired, 2019

"Because we are rapidly approaching a world with more and more sophisticated AI, we need to be the voices that shape how that AI ought to be used."

The computer that runs AlphaStar is a neural network that learns how to play video games similar to the way humans learn—except it has the time and capacity to watch and analyze thousands of games per day. The same company, DeepMind, also has a Neural Turing machine, which allows the neural network to access short-term memory similarly to humans. Because we are rapidly approaching a world with more and more sophisticated AI, we need to be the voices that shape how that AI ought to be used.

If AI becomes involved in more than organizing our shopping lists, they will begin to make life or death decisions. Robotic firefighters may have to choose who to save from a fire, and behind the AI, programmers will have to teach that AI what is right and what is wrong. More than ever before, humans are codifying, quite literally, what we believe to be ethical.

Even more so, when a future comes where wars are fought by robots, not humans, we need to be prepared to prime the discussion. Right now, the US military is testing AI-powered battlefield robots.[2] We need to be prepared to answer key questions: Is robot-based warfare even moral to begin with? Is moral culpability deferred just because we will no longer be sending our family and neighbors to fight wars? What happens when police forces are armed with robotic companions or replaced by robots in dangerous situations?

The questions are endless, but it is the church's responsibility to begin to think on these topics so that we are ready and prepared to be a valuable voice in the discussion on how new technologies ought to be used. Just like we do not need to be geneticists to understand and learn about the ethics of genetic modifications, we don't need to be computer scientists or engineers to be prepared to discuss the ethical ramifications of modern technology.

WHO AM I?

When we learn about the potential and terrifying applications of modern technology to warfare, we can begin to feel lost, scared, or even angry. However, when we face those sorts of reactions, we've already turned away from the burning bush. Instead of coming to God with curious questions, we've decided that the burning bush is far too terrifying, and we've walked away from God altogether.

When we come to these questions and begin to feel a loss of control or worry, we need to ask ourselves,

---

[2] *AI is accelerating the improvement of the US military's battlefield robots,* Teslarati, 2018

"When we embrace the answer that we are God's children, we can move forward without fear. We know that God is in control and that we can engage topics like these with thoughtful wisdom."

"Who am I?" Moses' question was not just a clarifying question, but it was a question that probed at his essential being. When we embrace the answer that we are God's children, we can move forward without fear. We know that God is in control and that we can engage topics like these with thoughtful wisdom.

In the 1940s, nuclear weapons were developed for the first time. Fear gripped the world as the horrors of Hiroshima and Nagasaki ended World War II. That fear continued to grip the conscious of the world for years until the end of the Cold War in 1991. Even as recently as the 2000s, the fear of Iran and North Korea creating nuclear weapons has weighed on the world.

However, there is no value in fear when we engage discussions of new, emerging technologies. When we choose to be paralyzed by fear, we cannot make valuable, informed mentoring decisions on how to view these technologies. The Catholic Church, for example, makes the statement that even possessing nuclear weapons is morally wrong.[3] But, are stances like this too simple to be valuable?

When we look at the role that nuclear weapons have played in the past decades, we may be tempted to say that they are morally reprehensible. However, it is difficult to understand how many wars they have prevented. Nuclear weapons ended the bloodiest war in human history, World War II, within which more than seventy million people died.[4] They also prevented the Cold War from becoming a real war.

Similarly, AI would reduce the number of casualties in war, but reduced moral behavior during wartime could be costly. AI Robots would be expensive, and their cost may be weighed against the lives of civilians. In addition, they could be used as an excuse to commit war crimes and blame the crime on the AI rather than the programmed or ordered behavior. AI may also not have the capacity to disobey immoral orders.

Instead of reacting to this development of technology with fear, it is important that we understand the direction that technology is going and embrace the valuable aspects of it without compromising our morals. Whether it is using Amazon's Alexa to play a song or the military employing AI powered robots, we need to remember that we are children of God, charged with the care of our world and our neighbors.

---

[3] *Where does the church stand on nuclear weapons,* U.S. Catholic, 2018

[4] Necrometrics

"Our goal is to be made into Christ's image, not to live comfortable and cushy lives. When we see comfort coming at the cost of others, we ought to tread carefully and fight for those who are being taken advantage of."

WHO SHOULD I TELL THEM SENT ME?

As Christians, we have been given something that the world lacks: Godly wisdom. If the world chooses to place profits over the privacy or safety of people, we need to be willing to use that wisdom to speak out for those who cannot speak for themselves. We have a duty to our neighbor, whether they are our geographical neighbor or not.

When it comes to explosive new technology like AI, we receive huge benefits of convenience, but we also need to recognize that convenience is not the goal of the life of a Christian. Our goal is to be made into Christ's image, not to live comfortable and cushy lives. When we see comfort coming at the cost of others, we ought to tread carefully and fight for those who are being taken advantage of.

Even in the space of digital advertising, there has been quite a buzz discussing whether or not big companies are using our smartphones to serve us ads.[5] When an emotional or frustrating event arises, if a phone is listening in, AI that power advertisements may be able to prey on people in weak moments to spend more than they ought to.

Even darker, the prospect of AI-powered war robots raises all sorts of human rights questions, especially if war has little human consequence for one side. The question of more frequent wars is not off the table if war becomes less expensive, in both monetary and human costs.

Due to the tendency to misuse technology, we need to be a voice of reason and moderation. We are equipped and sent by God to help those who are being taken advantage of, even if they don't know it. We ought to stand as a safeguard, mentoring those in our lives on the issues at hand.

We may not know any tech executives or military generals, but when the general population grabs ahold of something, they can make an impact. We need to treat our mentorship as a viral video, ready to come alive on its own and create a chain reaction. As we bring these ideas to light in the minds of those who haven't even considered them, we can help people prepare themselves for future discussions. Then, when we see predatory uses of AI, the world will be primed and ready to call it out.

---

[5]   *Is your smartphone listening to you?* BBC News, 2016

"Keeping our finger on the pulse of technology will help us to better direct those in our lives towards beneficial, new technologies and guide them away from destructive ones."

WHY SHOULD THEY LISTEN?

One of the biggest benefits of AI is how it can transform our lives. AI is poised to be the next refrigerator. It will help prevent and treat illness, it will be a source of convenience, and it will eventually change the face of the entire world. However, even refrigerators came with a cost, in the form of CFCs, or Chlorofluorocarbons, which are chemicals that have the potential to damage the ozone layer. AI, too, will bring costs, but we shouldn't throw the baby out with the bathwater.

When we come with the Godly wisdom afforded to us, we can uplift and uphold the beneficial parts of AI and condemn and reject the dangerous parts. When we research, think, and pray about the way new technology is developing, we can help guide it, through our discourse. Keeping our finger on the pulse of technology will help us to better direct those in our lives towards beneficial, new technologies and guide them away from destructive ones.

Instead of being afraid or ignorant of AI and other similar technological developments, we are able to, with study and attention, present the pros and cons of them to those around us. We don't need to be experts to thoroughly research and investigate what is going on in the world. When we give the time and attention that we ought to, we can make informed, ethical decisions and mentor those around us on how to discern the dangers in the technologies that are being presented to the world.

CHAPTER 6
Driverless Cars, Not Driverless Minds

> "The AI that power the driverless cars will have to make life and death decisions, and ultimately these will be influenced by the programmers who make them."

On Sunday, March 19th, 2018 a woman began walking her bike across the street. At the same time, a car was driving down the street. This car was special, because it didn't have a driver. Instead, it had an attendant whose job was to intervene if this driverless car ran into any issues. The attendant and the car did not see the woman, and at 10:00 p.m. that Sunday, the car struck and hit her. She died on impact.

As we see Artificial Intelligence technology progress, these types of situations will become an ever-present norm. We will also have to determine how these AI make decisions and who is at fault for them if they cause harm. Eventually, the road may be populated with driverless cars exclusively, but in the not-so-distant future we know we will see a time when drivers and driverless vehicles coexist.

As we see these scenarios grow, more questions and moral dilemmas will crop up. The AI that power the driverless cars will have to make life and death decisions, and ultimately these will be influenced by the programmers who make them.

CHAPTER 6

A simple scenario is one where a driver swerves into the lane of a driverless car. An elderly woman had tripped and fallen into the street, so the driver swerved, not seeing the driverless car coming around the bend. The driverless car sees that it is going to crash, so it is faced with a decision: it can swerve onto the sidewalk to avoid it or swerve into the other lane and hit the elderly woman lying on the ground. However, the driverless car also sees a young boy walking on the sidewalk. The driverless car can also choose to hit the other car head on, likely killing the passenger inside the driverless car and/or the driver of the other vehicle.

There is no simple solution to this problem. On that road, someone is going to die. However, that decision was made a long time ago. The decision was made by a programmer who decided that the AI should preserve youth over anything else. So, the driverless car will not hit the little boy. The driver of the other car is quite young herself. So, the driverless car chooses to kill the elderly woman.

In another scenario, the programmer's ethic was that survivability is the most important factor. The car can calculate who has the highest percentage of living in the event of a crash, so it chooses the boy on the side of the street. He is small and may run out of the way in time. So, the car blares it's horn, but the boy turns back, losing the precious second that he needed to run away to safety, and dies. The car chose the statistically best way to swerve, but the life of a young boy was ended that day.

The reality is, humans make these sorts of decisions in accidents as well. Often, a car may enter your lane and you have to swerve to avoid being hit, but you may hit someone coming up behind you. While we make these decisions, our reactions aren't programmed. In the case of driverless cars, someone has chosen ahead of time how the car will think about an accident scenario, and as Christians, it is our job to think about these things and be a voice in the conversation around them.

What we believe about life's essential value will come to the forefront when we discuss these topics, but we also need to remember that each person involved in the accident above was loved by someone. The driver may have been a married man, on his way to see his baby being born. The elderly woman may be the sole provider and caregiver for her grandchildren. The passenger in the driverless car could be a young daughter on her way to basketball practice, and the boy on the street is certainly beloved by his mother.

One might simply suggest that the first programmer was correct: We should preserve youth at any cost, but then the game changes. What if the elderly woman is a young boy darting out into the street? Now the oldest person in the scenario is the man going to witness the birth of his first child. In that scenario, that man dies.

Meanwhile, another might suggest that the second programmer was right: These accidents should be summed up by probability. But as we know, in that situation a young and innocent boy still dies. We have death no matter the scenario, and your opinion on the

---

"We ought to examine our values and preconceived notions to come to terms with how we view life and how it ought to be valued."

---

matter may change dramatically if that boy is your son or that woman is your grandmother.

As we explore this topic, we will find that many of these scenarios are no-win propositions. It can be tempting to suggest a "what if" scenario that saves everyone, but oftentimes, even a hyperintelligent AI is unable to react fast enough to save everyone. Instead, we ought to examine our values and preconceived notions to come to terms with how we view life and how it ought to be valued.

MOSES DRIVING THE CAR

Moses' role in the lives of the newly freed Israelites was primarily that of a guide. Moses physically guided the Israelites through the wilderness, and he also guided them spiritually. Moses' second recorded encounter with God was atop Mt. Sinai, and the encounter was not just for the benefit of Moses. God sent Moses down from the mountain with the Ten Commandments. The law contained in the Ten Commandments is vastly different from the temple law. The temple law has little to say on how to live a moral life and much more on how to live a life for temple worship.

The Ten Commandments were a guide, given to Moses to give to the people. Moses delivered those commandments and along with them a way of life that was God-honoring, respectful, honest, and good.

In a similar way, we are to offer Christ and the moral guidance that we received from Him to the world. When Christ summarizes the law, He summarizes as "Love the Lord your God with all your heart... and love your neighbor as yourself."[1] As we consider the moral gray areas that our technology may bring, it is important that we remember Christ's words and use them as a touchstone.

At some point, these programming decisions will become law, and Christians will need to be an informed and leading voice on the matter. It may not be in the next year or even five, but when the time comes, we ought to have a vested interest in these conversations for not only the safety of our loved ones, but also to help provide moral guidance. We ought to begin thinking about how we feel about these questions now and engage in fruitful conversation.

When we engage in these discussions, we aren't wasting time. Instead, we are taking the time to anticipate the real discussions we will ultimately have. When new technologies arise that ask us to make gray-area moral decisions, we will be more prepared. Even more than that, engaging in this type of thought

---

[1]   Luke 10:27

pattern will also help us to make decisions in the current gray-areas in our life.

DRIVING OUR MINDS

By cultivating an analytical mindset, we can create a mental environment that will help us any time we encounter difficult moral questions. When we consistently engage these types of analytical and moral problems, we will build important skills to help us through our lives.[2] When we develop these skills, we can more effectively care for those around us by becoming a moral authority.

This does not mean that we become pretentious, but instead, it means that we become guides for those around us. We can be mentors for those who are affected by changes in technology and maybe even robbed of loved ones. We can inform our politicians, local and beyond, and act as wise counsellors. Because we are equipped to take on these roles, we will raise ethical children, mentor ethical church members, and lift up ethical politicians.

When we take this type of grassroots approach to shape our world into a more moral one, we create an atmosphere of discourse and dialogue. We take the power away from those who seek to abuse it, and we can raise the need for strong dialogue about how we interact with technology that becomes more and more sophisticated and autonomous.

---

[2]   Proverbs 18:15

"What we want in our lives is driverless cars, not driverless minds."

What we want in our lives is driverless cars, not driverless minds. Alongside that, we need to reject the idea that these technologies are bad for us and that we should live in simpler times. When we understand the dangers that cars currently present us, we can come to the realization that driverless cars are a boon, even though they bring new moral questions.

New moral questions signal progress and advancement. Even alongside dangerous technologies like nuclear weapons, we have seen great gains from them. Nuclear energy, for example, is one of the cleanest forms of energy production, and it uses the least amount of land.[3] Though, there are a plethora of moral questions about nuclear weapons, the technology has created advantages, especially for countries like France that generates over 70% of it's energy via nuclear power.[4]

When we set aside our fear and engage new questions head on, we can separate the wheat from the chaff. We will be able to make valuable decisions and provide useful guidance. We also help others cultivate

---

[3]   *Air Quality,* Nuclear Energy Institute

[4]   *Why France Went Nuclear,* Clean Technica, 2014

"When we live our lives afraid of where our technology will take us, we become paralyzed."

---

a spirit of love, not a spirit of fear. When we live our lives afraid of where our technology will take us, we become paralyzed. When we are paralyzed by fear, we are unable to help affect our world positively and our role as ethical mentors is taken away from us.

CRITICAL THINKING AND THE ETHICAL MENTOR

Cultivating critical thinking skills is integral to our success as ethical mentors. Oftentimes, the situations that we will be called to mediate have unclear answers. It is our job to navigate murky situations and guide those in our lives towards what is good and true. To do this, we must first engage in discussions and thoughts that promote critical thinking. When we do this, we learn patterns that help us to preempt and adapt to new ethical dilemmas that we will face.

By making an attempt to preempt and engage with new technologies, we will be more than prepared for what the world throws at us. By being prepared instead of surprised, we can be a valuable voice in the lives of those around us.

Preparedness is also an act of love. Preparedness shows that we love not only those around us but ourselves as well. We are making proactive efforts to shape our world and to be valuable members of the church and our community.

CHAPTER 7
Technology and the Human Heart

Technology has helped humanity go to the moon and explore the depths of the oceans. In the future, it will better connect us and become faster and smarter, but with all of the benefits of technology, it is important that we understand how it affects us as human beings.

In 2010, 72% of teenagers in the United States had cell phones, and 25% of teenagers had access to social media on their phones.[1] This trend has done nothing but increase over the years. Coincidentally, in 2010 the number of incidents involving nonfatal self-harm in women ages ten to twenty-four that resulted in a hospital visit jumped. This is especially tragic as the trend continues to rise. In the past, these numbers had been quite stable, especially in the ten to fourteen-year-old category.

This meteoric rise in nonfatal self-harm in young, American women is enough to give anyone pause, but when researchers noticed the correlation between greater access to social media and self-harm many wondered about the correlation. Other studies have also found a link for both genders between the rise in suicide rates and social media usage.[2]

People are vying for love and acceptance, and many researchers believe that social media is damaging young people in that regard. When we see trends in self-harm and suicide among young people, it is important that we recognize how technology can

---

[1]   *Teens and Mobile Phones,* Pew Research Center, 2010

[2]   *Is Social Media Contributing to Rising Teen Suicide Rate?* NBC News, 2017

adversely affect our hearts. We also need to recognize the importance of guarding our hearts and mentoring others to guard their hearts, for we know that the heart is the wellspring of life.[3]

Technology offers many advantages, but as we can see it can also come with a great cost. It isn't necessarily our place to reject or push back against technology, but we must understand its uses and reject the detrimental effects that technology can bring.

What we see here more than anything is that we cannot look to technology as a cure for our broken hearts, or as thread used to stitch up those broken hearts. Today, the same as in the time of Caesar, human beings still want love and affection, and technology cannot replace or predict that.

Human beings will do the most illogical things because of their hearts. Some will die to save the life of a complete stranger and others will sacrifice their lives to set forth life changing ideology as we've seen over and over in the lives of the great women and men in history. Martin Luther King, Jr., Abraham Lincoln, Dietrich Bonhoeffer, Nelson Mandela, and Rosa Parks are examples.

No matter how technology grows, it cannot replace the parts of our lives that require human and divine connection. We cannot replace the urgings of the human heart with doctored social media perceptions and advertising.

---

[3]   Proverbs 4:23

Christianity will maintain its relevance because there will never come a point where the answers that Christianity gives will become obsolete. As we enter into this new age, it is important that we remember that Christianity is a valuable and eternal touchstone for truth and goodness.

Famously, C.S. Lewis commented once that "To be sure, the books of the future would be just as good a corrective as the books of the past, but unfortunately we cannot get at them." Lewis builds his case that it is important to look to the past more than we look at the present. What we can see through the lens of hindsight is that despite major changes in society and technology in the past one hundred years, Christianity has not become an ounce less valid or valuable.

THERE IS NOTHING NEW UNDER THE SUN

When we think of all of the records that are being broken in sports from swimming to high jump, we often rush to the conclusion that humans are progressing, getting better, stronger and faster. We might think the same thing when it comes to technology or education.

As we've seen, technology is growing at an amazing rate. One space that we hardly think of as "technology" is the realm of sports. However, recent examinations of the state of modern Olympic sports has given us some valuable insight on the state of progress of the human race.

CHAPTER 7

The 1908 Men's Olympic Marathon had a record time of two hours and fifty-five minutes. In 2016, the Winner of the Olympic Marathon did not set a record, but he completed the race in two hours and eight minutes. That is more than forty minutes of difference. One could quickly jump to the conclusion that humans have been getting faster or stronger over the last one hundred years.

Even in the realm of the mile race, in 1954, Sir Roger Bannister was the first man to run a mile in less than four minutes. But now, this is something that is standard for all male, professional middle-distance runners.

We can pull up countless examples of the records that have fallen over the years as athletes have reached greater heights. But oftentimes, we assume that the technology and infrastructure surrounding these scenarios are the same. One might even suggest, "He's running a race, how much different can it be? He has legs, doesn't he?"

However, as athletes will tell you, the equipment is an integral part of their success. In a recent TED talk,[4] David Epstein, a journalist, investigated the reasons for the advancements. When he consulted biomechanics experts, they mainly focused on the technology that was at play. For example, most races were run on cinders, not on soft, engineered tracks. When the resistance from the cinders was accounted for, many of the sub-four-minute mile times ended up being much higher.

---

[4]   *Are athletes really getting faster, better, stronger?* David Epstein, 2014

Even then, there have still been several hundred people since 1954 that have achieved these record times, and that is because people are training smarter and harder. Athletes have meal plans, workout schedules, and coaches. Sir Roger Bannister did not.

Technology has also impacted equipment, making it lighter and more aerodynamic. Even performance enhancing drugs have made their way into the Olympic scene, from steroids to blood doping.

All of that is to say that human beings have not changed much from one hundred years ago, a time when cars were new and refrigerators, as we know them, didn't exist. One of the ways that humanity has changed dramatically is its use of technology, not as a species. Humans along history have had the same innate intelligence, athletic ability, and emotions as we have now.

When we consider all of this, it helps us ground ourselves and understand that there is, as Ecclesiastes says, "nothing new under the sun."[5] We see that humans, despite all the ways that we have changed the world around us, have maintained the same essence.

---

[5]   Ecclesiastes 1:9 NIV

THE URGINGS OF THE HUMAN HEART

One of humanity's fundamental desires is to be loved. When Moses asks the Lord in the burning bush "Who am I?" He is admitting that the Israelites hold no love for him, and he is admitting that he is inadequate. In our modern world, that is why this question resonates so deeply with us.

In a world seeking love, we often look to technology to fill that void. We try to protect ourselves from feelings of worthlessness by projecting an illusory life. When people seek love from people online, they are trying to fill an unfillable void. When people project themselves as something contrary to their real life on social media, they are trying to generate local fame and are lying to themselves. More now than ever, humanity is taking to technology to try to replace what they can't attain for themselves. People post flattering photos on social media with the intention of accumulating likes and comments instead of using social media as a way to connect with and encourage those around them.

There is nothing inherently evil about the technology of social media, but trying to create an internet persona for other people to fall in love with leaves us shriveled up as people. People don't fall in love with us but, instead, with the carefully crafted image that we present online.

Moses' second question unveils a second fundamental desire of humanity. "Who should I tell them sent me?" is a question that many people pour their lives into because it is a question of identity and self-value. Oftentimes, people choose to be identified by what they do or how they feel rather than who they are. The desire of athletes to be the pinnacle of human athleticism often causes them to engage in illegal or dangerous acts and take risks by utilizing steroids or blood doping.

The question begs a specific kind of answer. Hidden in the question is, "Who are you that anyone should care?" When Moses asks this question of God, he is asking God to provide him with authority and power. When Moses receives his answer, that certainly comes. However, when we ask the same questions without looking to receive our authority and power from God, we will inevitably find ourselves striving for nothing.

Any fame or value that we gain of ourselves is fleeting and meaningless, and we can only obtain meaning by generating things of eternal value. As humans, our desire for value and meaning can only flourish into something real if it takes root in God. Otherwise, we are just asking for the praise of men.[6]

Moses' last question, "Why should they listen?" highlights the deep-seated insecurity of trying to gain value and worth in worldly ways. When we fail to realize that our meaning and power is rooted in Christ, we will quietly ask ourselves why anyone cares. It is in this place that we turn to self-promotion and self-indulgence. It is the same fear of failure or inadequacy that leads people to depression and to use performance enhancing drugs. It is the same fear that

---

[6]   John 12:43

drives people to edit their photos and post them on social media.

When we act out of fear, rather than trust of who God is, we are doomed to fail. We will find ourselves scrambling for affirmation. As time goes on, we realize that the affirmation won't come, and we will be lost.

Because of the way the human heart seeks to find it's worth, we can never find the answers to what we seek in technology. We can use technology to help us better ourselves, do good things, and bring glory to God. However, when we seek to use technology to fill the void in our hearts, we will never be satisfied.

MENTORING THE HUMAN HEART

As we guide ourselves and those around us, it is imperative that we remember that we are mentoring human beings, beloved by God. When we nurture a healthy relationship with those whom we mentor, we can help them to avoid the pitfalls of searching for the desires of their hearts in the wrong places.

We can help others learn how to integrate technology properly into their new lives, not accept or reject it wholesale. We can teach them to be athletes that use technology to propel themselves forward, not people addicted to social media for approval.

When we mentor as a relationship, not as a task or goal, we can help others find their fulfillment in a model of the relationship between God and mankind. We can use our mentoring relationships to point others to God simply by being a friend who uplifts and guides. When those we mentor see the value of this earthly relationship, the context of a heavenly relationship becomes clearer.

Consider how hard it is for a person who has had an abusive or absent father to understand God's role as Heavenly Father. It is equally as difficult for those who have created false relationships with technology and other humans to understand God as our friend. So, mentoring is a means by which we reveal God and a means by which we shape both ours and others' relationships with technology.

By taking the time to meet with others face-to-face, we are showing them how valuable they are and emulating God's relationship with us. Taking time is an act of sacrifice on our part, and the act itself speaks volumes. The human heart longs to be accepted and valued, and regardless of someone's appearance, race, disability, or sexual orientation, we can help heal the scars caused by the misuse of technology. But we must realize that this healing can only take place when we make the sacrifices necessary to experience those face-to-face moments with the friends and mentees in our lives.

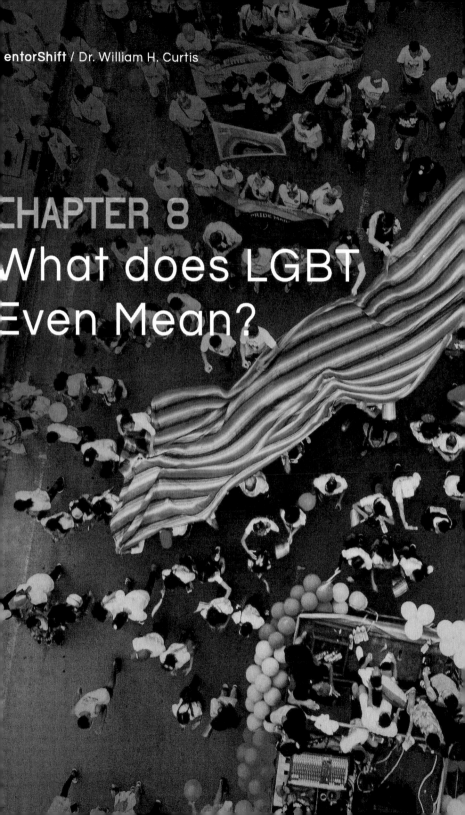

CHAPTER 8
What does LGBT Even Mean?

Over the past few decades, homosexuality, gender, and the church has become a hot debate. About 4.7% of Americans identify as LGBT,[1,2] and this comparatively small group of people has caused one of the biggest stirs in Christianity in recent times. Some Christians have come to the conclusion that homosexuality is not named as sin in the bible, whereas others have maintained that the Bible names homosexuality as a sin.

The question of this debate is even more deeply complicated by the T at the end of LGBT. Transgenderism is even more rarely discussed than homosexuality. About 0.58% of Americans identify as transgender,[3] and that is a percentage so low that some of us do not even know someone who identifies as such.

Some people may be tempted to assert that small outliers like the LGBT population, and especially the transgender population, do not necessitate wide-ranging debate and implementation of rules and laws meant to regulate the treatment of the LGBT community. As Christians, we are charged to show compassion to those around us and to model our lives after the example that Jesus set. As Philippians 2:1-4 says, "Therefore if you have any encouragement from

---

[1] *In U.S., Estimate of LGBT Population Rises to 4.5%,* Gallup 2018

[2] LGBT, or Lesbian, Gay, Bisexual, and Transgender, is shorthand for any of those who find themselves affiliated with that community and is not limited to those specific terms.

[3] *How Many Adults Identify as Transgender in the United States?* The Williams Institute, 2016

being united with Christ, if any comfort from his love, if any common sharing in the Spirit, if any tenderness and compassion, then make my joy complete by being like-minded, having the same love, being one in spirit and of one mind. Do nothing out of selfish ambition or vain conceit. Rather, in humility value others above yourselves, not looking to your own interests but each of you to the interests of the others."[4]

The conversation about the LGBT community and the church is not an easy one, but it is an important one. This conversation is one that weighs on many church members, and it is important for us to understand why.

For some, this conversation is heavy enough for them to leave the church altogether, so it is our duty to explore this topic with due diligence. If we approach the topic of LGBT and the church with a sense that we already know all of the answers, we are pushing away people that are seeking out a place of refuge, compassion, and in some sense, understanding. Instead, it is imperative that we engage in the conversation with open hearts and minds, listening to all sides of the argument and then making decisions that are scripturally grounded and based on the answer to the question: What would Jesus do? It is also important that we don't have insular conversations amongst ourselves, but instead interface with members of the LGBT community. Only then can we come to a clearer and more loving understanding of the topic.

---

4   Philippians 2:1-4 NIV

"If we do not try to understand what makes us different, why it makes us different, and how this intersects with our faith, we will have great difficulty in mentoring and helping others on their journey of healing through Christ."

The debate about the LGBT community is contentious because of love. For the LGBT community, they want to be able to love whomever they would like, and they believe that the church's efforts to block that has been devastating to them. For the LGBT community, they are being asked to shelve what they believe to be one of their most innate biological desires for the sake of their Christianity. For the transgender community, they are asked to love the very bodies that they hate.

Even if you are part of a church that affirms LGBT individuals, past scars are not always fully healed. Because of this, we need to approach conversations with the LGBT community, especially Christian LGBT individuals, with a deep sense of compassion and with an open mind, aiming to understand the plight within which they live.

If we do not try to understand what makes us different, why it makes us different, and how this intersects with our faith, we will have great difficulty in mentoring and helping others on their journey of healing through Christ.

WHO AM I?

When God sent Moses to the Israelites, one of his primary questions was "Who am I, that I should go unto Pharaoh, and that I should bring forth the children of Israel out of Egypt?" In a very similar way, the church today has been asking God the same question about the LGBT community.

The challenge before us as mentors of not only heterosexual but LGBT individuals is not one that we should take lightly. The challenges that the LGBT community faces, regardless of opinion on its sinfulness, is something that you may have no understanding of. However, it is our divine duty as Christians to love our neighbors. When we commit to this first, we can then enter into relationship with members of the LGBT community.

Only within the context of relationship can we hope to affect the lives of our LGBT brothers and sisters. This is precisely what Moses did to regain the trust of the Israelites, and it was hard won. Initially, Moses came with God's power, and the twelve signs that God performed opened Pharaoh's eyes. Pharaoh was convinced, but the Israelites were not. Soon after the Israelites escaped Egypt, they began to complain about a lack of food, and even suggested that it would have been better if they would have died in Egypt.[5]

---

[5] Exodus 16:3

Moses had his work cut out for him, but he chose to persevere, and with God's help, he took the time to build up his relationship with the Israelites. Through God, he delivered mana, water, the Ten Commandments, temple law, and at his death, brought them to the edge of the promised land. Similarly, we can, through God's help, build a trusting relationship between ourselves and the LGBT individuals that we mentor.

Only in the context of a relationship can we have the important conversations that this topic requires. When we begin to have these conversations, we can affect and engage the lives of this group and begin to mend the bridges that have been burned. Without the context of a relationship, we cannot hope to mentor anyone.

Part of creating a relationship is to enter it with a level of mutual respect. Just like Moses was actively involved in the daily lives of the Israelites, we too need to get our hands dirty in our relationships with our mentees who are LGBT. We cannot approach this relationship with the idea that somehow heterosexuals are better or more holy. By giving them room to express their opinions, not only do we change their perspective on us, but we also learn how to be better conversationalists. We can challenge and expand our own views and engage in new ideas on any topic. This type of listening will help us to engage rather than preach and will help our relationships to become valuable to both parties.

WHO SHOULD I TELL THEM SENT ME?

The Bible tells us that on Pentecost the disciples gathered, "were filled with the Holy Spirit and spoke the word of God boldly."[6] In modern Christianity, it is often reinforced that we are to be bold and unashamed by our faith. There are plenty of scriptures to back up this way of practicing our faith, and there is nothing wrong with boldness. However, as the author of Ecclesiastes championed, there is a time and place for everything.[7]

When God sent Moses, He sent Moses with the name of God as his vanguard. Moses boldly went to Pharaoh, but Pharaoh's first response to him was precisely what Moses feared. Pharaoh said, "Who is the LORD that I should obey His voice and let Israel go? I do not know the Lord, and besides, I will not let Israel go."[8]

Despite coming with the name of the Lord, Pharaoh had no respect or interest in what Moses had to say and sent him away. Not only that, but Pharaoh increased the burden on the Israelites. Then, the foremen of the Israelites came to Moses and Aaron and told them, "May the LORD look upon you and judge you, for you have made us odious in Pharaoh's sight and in the sight of his servants, to put a sword in their hand to kill us."[9]

---

6   Acts 4:31 NIV

7   Ecclesiastes 3:1

8   Exodus 5:2 NIV

9   Exodus 5:21 NASB

"We are to enter into a relationship of service to our LGBT brethren to win them to Christ. It is not our role to change them, but rather it is the divine role of the Almighty God to bring them into Christ-likeness."

Ultimately, the Lord delivers His revenge upon Pharaoh, but if we think that simply telling people that we are Christians and boldly professing our faith is the solution to every evangelical and relational problem, we have deluded ourselves. If we confuse friends for enemies, we treat the Israelites in our lives like the Pharaohs of our lives.

Instead, it is imperative that we maintain a relationship with the LGBT community. We are not Moses coming to bring the plagues, we are Paul writing to Philemon. Philemon is one of the most unique books of the new testament, wherein Paul sends Onesimus, his friend so beloved he calls him a son, back to his former master, Philemon, with this letter in hand. While Paul has no intention of forcing Philemon to accept Onesimus as a dear brother rather than a servant, he says, "I could be bold and order you to do what you ought to, yet I prefer to appeal to you on the basis of love."[10]

---

[10]   Philemon 1:8 NIV

Similarly, we are to offer ourselves to the LGBT community not as bold Christians commanding reformation, but instead as humble servants, just as Paul said, "For though I am free from all, I have made myself a servant to all, that I might win more of them."[11]

We are to enter into a relationship of service to our LGBT brethren to win them to Christ. It is not our role to change them, but rather it is the divine role of the Almighty God to bring them into Christ-likeness.

Oftentimes, our Christian culture presses us to be judgmental and controlling, pointing out sin in the lives of those around us. However, in the case of those who have felt immense hurt at the hands of some members of the church, we are to be especially loving, even unto self-sacrifice. As mentors, our goal is not temporal but eternal. When we love unto hurting, we can affect the lives of estranged individuals in ways that we cannot fathom.

Only in the context of love, not boldness, can we demonstrate what one ought to do. We cannot show the LGBT community the truth of Jesus Christ without love. If we command them in boldness or condemn them from afar, we have succeeded in nothing more than pushing them further from theirs and the world's only source of healing, Jesus Christ.

---

[11] 1 Corinthians 9:19 ESV

"As we enter into relationship, we gain the right to be heard, but we also gain the obligation to listen."

WHY SHOULD THEY LISTEN?

When we contribute a valuable and powerful friendship and mentorship to someone's life, we gain credibility and validity in their eyes. Without this context, it is impossible to speak difficult truths to someone and see those truths take root in someone's life. If we do not enter into relationship, they certainly will not listen.

Had Moses' attempts to free the Israelites been nothing more than vain speech, they would have no reason to revere Moses. If Moses' life had not been so intimately involved in the lives of the Israelites, he would not be the greatest of the prophets. In the same way, without the context of a personal relationship, the LGBT community has no reason to listen to Christianity's teachings. In many cases, Christianity is antithetical to how they live their lives every day, and to accept those teachings is to give up their whole life.

As we enter into relationship, we gain the right to be heard, but we also gain the obligation to listen. This give and take of a relationship is the only context within which we can become the vehicles of Christ's healing, and part of that is to listen to the pain and hurt of others. When we do this, we can begin to bridge the divides that history has created.

THE ETHICAL MENTOR AND THE LGBT MENTEE

As mentors, relationship is key and that means that we have a responsibility to understand the struggles of our mentees. As we find ourselves mentoring LGBT individuals, it is important to understand that each individual has a different experience. There is a profound difference between the experience of a gay individual and a transgender individual, and that means that we have to approach each mentoring relationship individually.

A transgender individual, for example, may not consider themselves gay or lesbian if they date someone who has a gender opposite of their new identity. A gay, lesbian, bisexual, or other individual may have different experiences of faith and lifestyle. Some LGBT members of the church may maintain celibate lives and will require a different kind of mentorship and support structure than someone who believes that their LGBT status is not sinful.

As such, when we engage these individuals, it is important to take time to listen and show that we care. When we take that time and make a concerted effort to understand life from the viewpoint of those we mentor, we can better pour into their lives and we can also better prepare their hearts to be open to the power of Christ.

One of the most important parts of this mentor-mentee relationship is that we do not judge or condemn, but instead we act as an arrow that continually points to Christ. If we accomplish this, we can rest in Christ's power that He is mighty to save. It is not our duty to save, but it is Christ's alone. When we relinquish that duty and return it, rightfully, to Christ, then we can find that we can become a valuable mentor to those around us.

CHAPTER 9
It's Not All in Your Head

Humanity's relationship with mental health has a long and complex history. Ancient history has treated conditions of the brain such as epilepsy as "sacred"[1] and believed that those exhibiting symptoms of schizophrenia possessed special abilities and insight. Oftentimes, those that exhibited these symptoms, even if due to mental illness, would be raised up as oracles and seers in their respective societies.

In the 1800s, a theory, therapeutic nihilism, took hold. It argued that many cures do more harm than good, especially for those diagnosed with a mental illness. However, this ultimately faded away, as medical education began to standardize and reform. But, in the 1940s, 50s, and 60s, psychiatric hospitals were performing over a thousand lobotomies per year until the practice nearly disappeared in the 1970s. From the 1970s to the present, mental health has become better understood and breakthroughs in psychiatry and medicine have helped us to better understand these conditions.[2]

As science progresses and mental illness is better understood, it is important that we as Christians are keeping up with that science as well. We might not be therapists, psychiatrists, or social workers, but we are called to serve those in need, and that includes those living with mental illness. To do this, it is important for us to create church-wide

---

[1]   On the Sacred Disease, Hippocrates

[2]   Mental Health Services Then and Now, David Mechanic, 2007

programs that directly support these individuals in our congregations and communities.

With churches providing services and events that are generally open to the public, individuals experiencing mental health challenges can easily walk through the doors of a church and become involved in church communities. Many churches report that they know large numbers of people who live with mental illness,[3] but studies have shown that "only 12.5% of church leaders say that mental illness is discussed openly and in a healthy way within their church."[4] However, with many church leaders being approached for help in handling situations involving someone living with mental illness,[5] it is important to take proactive steps to help those who suffer.

When we take the time to create programs and procedures for those living with mental health issues, not only are we helping, but we are also creating a safer environment for them, ourselves, and our churches. We must endeavor to treat those living with mental illness as Christ did. Christ made a habit out of eating and sitting with those who were in some way shunned or seen as "less than" by society. Thus, it is important for us to balance the way we run our ministries to ensure a certain level of comfort for parishioners along with compassion and humane treatment for those with a

---

[3] *The Church and Mental Health: What Do the Numbers Tell Us?* Christianity Today, 2018

[4] *Troubled Minds: Mental Illness and the Church's Mission,* Amy Simpson, 2013

[5] Ibid

mental health challenge. When we take the time to consider, plan, and train, we can create healing and respectful environments.

WHO AM I?

For those living with a mental illness, the question "Who Am I?" may take on a different tone. Some mental illnesses erode at one's sense of identity. Others destroy one's sense of worth. When we consider the question "Who am I?" it is important that we recognize God's implicit answer to Moses when Moses asked this question.

God knew that Moses was a murderer. He knew he was an exile, not just of Egypt but of the Israelites. Many people living with a mental illness feel exiled or unwanted, whether perceived or true. We can see this explicitly in the homeless population, where twenty to twenty-five percent of the homeless suffer from a severe mental illness.[6] For the general population, this is closer to four percent, but that means that one in twenty-five people will suffer from a serious mental illness. If your church has at least twenty-five members, one of those members may be suffering from a mental illness.

Because a person with a mental health diagnosis can often feel alone or helpless, it is important that we have support structures in place to support them. It is also

---

[6]   *Mental Illness and Homelessness,* National Coalition for the Homeless, 2009

important that we reinforce the message that God gave Moses at the burning bush: In spite of Moses' status as an exile, God still chose him and chose to raise him up. Even though he wasn't equipped as a speaker, God still choose him, even over his brother Aaron. Individuals living with a mental illness, likewise, are not exiled from God's promise. It is our responsibility to communicate that to them and to uplift them, in spite of their struggle.

By reinforcing their self-worth, we can contribute to the spiritual healing that they need, even if we are unable to personally contribute to their mental healing. It is important, too, that we don't try to treat their illness simply with Christian kindness.

As beneficial as that is, mental health issues require a professional hand. It is important for us to understand when we have reached our personal limits as mentors and friends. To be a valuable mentor and friend, we must be able to refer those around us to more capable hands. A friend may not be able to help you with a plumbing issue, but they may know a reputable plumber to refer you to. Similarly, we can be a better friend by referring someone to a professional that we or others in our network recommend.

Moses understood that he was not a public speaker, and even used that excuse with God, but God knew better. God understood that Moses was the right person for the job, but also understood that Aaron had a role to play in that success as well. Our role is similar. We can be the ambassador that connects those we mentor to mental health professionals. By acting as a bridge, just as Aaron did between Moses and the people, we can better help those that we encounter that are living with a mental health condition.

When we understand our limitations, we can better help our mentees and friends. Understanding our own limitations helps us to not only better ourselves, but to uplift and empower others. Just as an arm can't take the role of an eye, those of us who are not trained to be mental health professionals cannot take on that role. We can only act to empower those with that gift and training.

WHO SHOULD I TELL THEM SENT ME?

Mental illness is unlike physical illness in many ways. When you break your arm, it is clear what is causing the problem, it is clear where the pain is coming from, and it is clear what the solution is. You go to the doctor, he or she gives you some pain killers and a cast and sends you and your now itchy arm on its way for a few weeks, and then when you return, the cast is cut off.

With a mental illness, the solution is not always easy or straight forward. In the past, people were simply shunned and locked away or, even worse, lobotomized or given painful, dangerous therapies. Now, treatment of a mental illness can require much more guesswork and trial and error than many expect. There is no way to cure depression outright, for example, with a standardized cocktail of drugs. Everyone's brain chemistry is different. It can require a great deal of not only trial and error, but patience and pain for someone

---

"If we hope to see healing in the lives of our mentees, we need to make it clear that God is with them, even if they are not healed."

---

with a mental health condition to find a treatment that provides them with the ability to simply live their life.

Similarly, we cannot promise those who live with a mental illness that Christ will suddenly change their situation or cure their condition. He may, and He has that power, but it is important that we remember that He alone is in charge of that power, not us. If we hope to see healing in the lives of our mentees, we need to make it clear that God is with them, even if they are not healed. And, there are some who only find healing after this life. We need to maintain patience and love for those in our lives that are living with a mental illness.

It is easy to lash out or lose patience when those we have let into our lives disappoint us, relapse, or have uncontrollable reactions to their illness. God has called us to be His ambassadors, however, and patiently work with the people in our lives, in spite of their condition. Moses was given charge over the Israelites, but it is clear that they tried and tested his patience. Moses wasn't ashamed that he struggled to be patient with the Israelites, but he took great efforts to maintain his composure and control.

When Moses did not maintain his composure, he found himself in deep trouble. Moses had just buried his sister Miriam, and the Israelites fought with Moses and complained that he had offered them nothing but death. God provided provision for the Israelites by asking Moses to strike a rock and from that rock water would come forward. But Moses, in his anger, struck the rock twice, berating the Israelites while he did so.[7]

God punished Moses for this act because Moses did not trust God in the face of struggle and did not showcase God's holiness before the Israelites. This act stopped Moses from entering the promised land.

We can learn from this encounter how important it is to be models of God's holiness and patience when we interact with those we mentor and have relationships with. If we stumble, the consequences are not just for ourselves, but set a bad example for those who need the example the most. It is important that we maintain our composure because if we cannot reflect God's heart and we fail to recognize the importance of others, no matter their struggle, then we fail to embody God's own qualities.

WHY SHOULD THEY LISTEN?

Many people with mental illness fail to seek or receive treatment, with rates as low as thirty-two percent for schizophrenia and as high as seventy-eight percent for alcohol dependence. There are many reasons for this,

---

[7]   Numbers 20:1-13

from social stigma, unwillingness to admit that there is something wrong, fear of drug-related side effects, and lack of access to adequate insurance to pay the costs associated with some medications and treatments.

For those with a mental illness, treatment can be as frightening as the illness itself. It can involve new, terrifying drugs or a stay in a privacy-devoid hospital, oftentimes with people who have much more complicated mental health conditions. The entire experience of seeking and receiving treatment can be a traumatizing one, so the question, "Why should they listen?" when we urge them to get help is powerfully poignant.

The answer to this question is a long, involved one. It is not a simple, pithy answer. Those who are suffering from a mental illness have many reasons not to listen. Because of this, it is important that we, as leaders in the church, take a proactive step to build programs that support and help our friends and congregants who suffer.

Many churches do not have a mental health ministry, and churches sometimes propagate dangerous stigmas that surround mental health. This is a terrifying prospect when we consider that a member of clergy is usually the first person that someone goes to when they have a mental health issue.[8] Because this is often out of the scope of pastoral training, pastors can feel unprepared. This is often doubly so for lay leaders.

---

[8] *Patterns and Correlates of Contacting Clergy for Mental Disorders in the United States,* Health Services Research, 2003

"The prospect of creating a mental health ministry is a challenging one, but it is important that we strive to develop and strategize ministries that target such a large portion of our congregations."

However, we cannot fail in our duty to love and serve even if the prospect is a difficult one. The prospect of creating a mental health ministry is a challenging one, but it is important that we strive to develop and strategize ministries that target such a large portion of our congregations.

When we step out and make our churches and lives a safe, healthy space for those who are suffering, we can show them why they should listen. We can show them the patience of Christ and His willingness to come alongside each and every one of His children. By treating our brothers and sisters living with a mental health condition as humans in need and not diseases or diagnoses, we will find the gumption to divert our time and resources to help them.

Relationship can help us overcome any of the latent prejudices that we may have as well. When we begin to pore into the lives of others and begin to care about them, the way we see them shifts. We no longer see them as addicts or crazy people. Instead, we understand their struggle through shared conversation and understand how to better engage them.

CREATING A MENTAL HEALTH MINISTRY

Creating a mental health ministry can be difficult, especially for a small church or for an individual. However, the need is so great that these ministries are becoming essential parts of the church. It is important that the church keeps ahead of this curve and that church leaders view those living with a mental health issue as brothers and sisters in Christ, not untouchables or unwanted.

One of the biggest challenges to creating a mental health ministry can be getting started. However, it doesn't need to be much more than a support group, a place where those living with a mental illness can discuss their struggles in a group with mutual understanding. Often these safe places are invaluable, as it can be terribly difficult to discuss inner struggles, especially with mind-altering conditions. Even those with depression and anxiety may find themselves unable to discuss their inner struggles.

This should not replace professional services, but act as an augmentation to those services. While creating these meetings, it may be helpful to contact a local psychiatrist, therapist or counselor to determine how to best tailor these meetings. This also provides you with opportunities to develop relationships with trustworthy and valuable mental health professionals so that you can refer those within your congregation that may have this need. Even if your church doesn't have a mental health professional on staff or in the congregation, it is important that you connect with local resources.

It is also wise to take advantage of free programs that educate on mental health issues. A good example would be Mental Health First Aid, which hosts free classes that help prepare people to be good first responders in the event of a mental health crisis. Mental health ministries also have to deal with some of the most raw and human parts of our world, and this includes suicide. Being prepared to deal with this is incredibly important, and learning warning signs and how to appropriately contact the correct responders can save lives.

Without relationship, it is difficult to develop empathy that leads to patience. By taking the time to create programs, become educated, and involve ourselves in real relationships, we can create a new church culture around mental illness that will supersede and replace the stigma of the past.

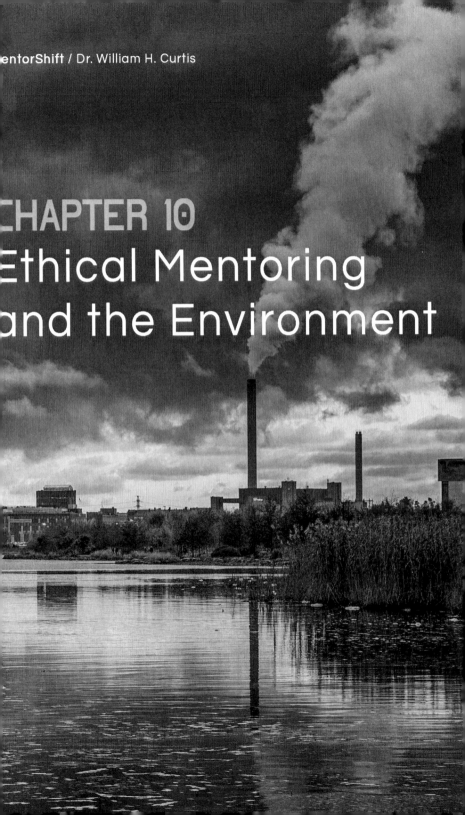

CHAPTER 10
Ethical Mentoring
and the Environment

In the 2006 documentary *An Inconvenient Truth*, the world was reminded of the importance of the environment. In the film, Al Gore shows slide after slide, packed with data that shows the perilous state of our climate and ecosystem. One of Gore's key points in this documentary is that many of the long-held ideas that we have had about our world have been proven to be false.

Similarly, the view that we as humans have little to no bearing on our environment is being proven false day by day. Even if we ignore the idea of climate change, pollution has steadily increased, and our habits concerning our garbage have created massive landfills.

One of the biggest sources of our ignorance is how well hidden all of this has become. In April of 2019, China banned the import of foreign garbage to curb pollution, and the world quickly became aware of what was happening with their trash. Few people knew that the paper plates and plastic forks that they were throwing away were being sent half way around the world to countries like China to sit in mountain-sized landfills.[1] Even more, giant, country-sized pools of garbage are piling up in the Pacific Ocean and drenching the beaches of tropical paradises like the Dominican Republic.[2]

---

[1]   *The world is scrambling now that China is refusing to be a trash dumping ground,* CNBC, 2018

[2]   *Wave after Wave of Garbage Hits the Dominican Republic,* The New York Times, 2018

While this truth may be inconvenient, it is not something that we can continue to ignore. Our trash is so unlike the garbage of the 18th and 19th centuries. Our plastics, created to be long-lasting and durable, have proven to be exactly that. These plastics are building up in our oceans, on the sides of our streets, and even in our food.[3]

With this in mind, it is of the utmost importance that we take this environmental crisis seriously. Our responsibility as mentors and leaders is to aggressively counsel and teach others the importance of our environment. Even the most fatalistic Christians can understand our God-given role to steward creation and help ensure a healthy world for those who come after us.

As we show the importance of the environment to those that we mentor, we can help reinforce healthy ways of interacting with the environment. We do not need to encourage people to extricate themselves from the environment, but rather we ought to teach them to live as a part of it. When we learn healthy ways of interacting with the environment, we will be able to exemplify them for others.

IN THE BEGINNING

During the ages of evangelism to and colonization of the African Continent, one of the major errors of the Christians who came to Africa was to misinterpret

---

[3]   *Are Microplastics in Food a Threat to Your Health?* Healthline, 2018

Africa's monotheistic tendencies. African religious beliefs were often classified as polytheistic and primitive. However, the indigenous African cultures considered God to be omnipresent in nature.

For many African cultures, this translated into a respectful view of life in general, not just human life, and they strove to protect it at all costs. Where Western society has gone wrong is that we have tried to remove God's presence from the environment and consider it to be nothing more than a tool for mankind to use to our own ends.

In the first Chapter of Genesis, God declares that the whole of creation is "very good."[4] The universe is God's handiwork, and as such He cares about it deeply. We sin against the earth now more than ever. Humanity has taken on a negative view of the world, seeking not to care for our world[5] but to subjugate it. By seeking to use the world to our benefit, even unto its or our own detriment, we have abused the good and perfect gift that God has put plainly before us.

We have an obligation to reclaim our God-given command to care for the earth. This ethical imperative is something that is so far removed from our normal conversations that we do not even consider it to be something worth mentoring others on. We may think that environmentalism is important or that we ought to do more, but there are many instances where this is nothing more than lip-service or wishful thinking.

---

[4]   Genesis 1:31

[5]   Genesis 2:15

As Christians, it is our duty to personally reform our environmental practices, advise our government and leaders to do the same, and also teach those who we mentor the spiritual and practical importance of environmental care.

When we fail to rise to this responsibility, we allow planet altering and life changing disasters like the BP Oil Spill of 2010. Even to this day, pockets of oil still exist in the Gulf of Mexico, especially in the marshes and estuaries on the coast.[6] However, very little consequence came for those responsible for the spill. Overall, BP paid a total of $62 billion for the oil spill, but it is difficult to know how far reaching the impacts of the spill are.

With this disaster in mind, we ought to push for safer alternatives to oil, especially when we see a push for fracking by similar companies. Many people, especially those with private wells, have found that fracking has created pollution in their water sources and toxic gases are often let out into the air we breathe during the process.[7]

Ultimately, by caring for our earth, we are caring for ourselves. By encouraging those around us to explore safer, cleaner alternatives, we are embodying God's love of His creation and paving the way for those that will be born generations after us to experience God's creation as He intended.

---

[6]   *Gulf of Mexico Oil Spill,* Smithsonian

[7]   *Fracking is Dangerous to Your Health — Here's Why,* Forbes, 2017

WHO AM I?

As human beings, we have a special place as environmental advocates. Not only are we sentient, logical, and the most powerful species on the planet, but we are also imbued with God's spirit and charged to look after creation. Even more, we are a part of the environment. Though we may not consider it, we deal with the effects of dangerous weather, enjoy beautiful sunny days, and breathe air. We are not disembodied minds, but we are bodies in our environment. We may live in a safe and clean area, but we often fail to realize how our environmental decisions affect others, including plants and animals that we rely on.

When we look to Moses as an example, we may think that Moses had little to say about the environment. However, Moses's story is not simply one of Moses freeing the Israelites in the abstract. Instead, Moses and the Israelites took a long, arduous journey through the wilderness, the harshest of environments.

We may be tempted to ignore the fact that the Israelites traveled through the wilderness for forty years and that they struggled to find food and potable water during their journey. The story of the Exodus is not simply a great struggle against Egypt and a great struggle against the Canaanites. The majority of the Exodus was a great struggle with the environment.

Environment is an often overlooked but central part of the whole of the Old Testament. First, Adam and Eve were taken from the Garden of Eden, the perfect environment, overflowing with beauty and sustenance. Then, Abraham journeyed with his wife and children through the wilderness to what would eventually become Israel. A famine came and forced the Israelites out and into Egypt where they found themselves enslaved.

When the Israelites journeyed through the wilderness, they were exposed to the harshness of the environment and also to the fragility of it. Their goal was the "land of milk and honey," the Promised Land. We can learn from the Exodus that the environment is something that God expects us to intimately relate to and something through which God reveals Himself to us. God formed Adam from the dust of the ground. He also formed every other living, breathing thing from the dust of the ground.[8]

God speaking to Moses through a burning bush was not a frivolous choice. Instead, it brings up echoes of Christ's light coming into the world—the material world. When we apply this to what John says of Christ in the New Testament, we understand that "For God so loved the world" means that He loves the environment as well.

The word, "world" is kosmos in the original language. It denotes the entire universe, not simply earth. When we consider that God loved the world enough to send Christ to it, we then understand that God's love is not just for us humans, but for every atom of our universe. This is precisely because it is His creation.

---

[8]   Genesis 2:18

WHO SHOULD I TELL THEM SENT ME?

One of the key details that we can learn from the West's misunderstanding of traditional African monotheism is that connection to nature can help connect us to God. When we look at the world around us and consider it as a created thing that God called "good," we begin to develop a much greater respect for it.

It is easy for us to forget that we live in a technologically advanced, material world. What many of us drive in an hour would have taken our ancestors days to traverse. We cross over once impassable rivers and through tunnels in mountains and hills. We often fail to even recognize that we are doing so. This has changed dramatically in the past one hundred years, as even one hundred years ago, people came to America on boats, not on planes.

The Israelites traversed the wilderness for forty years before they reached the Promised Land—Israel. However, the distance from Cairo to Jerusalem is about a seven-hour drive. Walking it wouldn't even take a month, let alone forty years. However, God wanted to teach the Israelites something on their way to the Promised Land, the land of milk and honey.

The terrain was tough and sparse and there was a lack of water and food in the wilderness. But God took the Israelites into that desolate place to show them the importance of devotion to Him. Without reliance and devotion to God, the Israelites had no hope of driving out the people who had taken up residence in

Israel, and the Israelites couldn't come to rely on God without struggle.

By the end of their forty years, the Israelites had experienced some great things, and a new generation of Israelites, who had not known Egypt began to enter their new Eden—Israel. Much like the Israelites, those of us living in first-world countries have arrived at this present and hitherto unknown level of comfort and luxury on the backs of many wilderness wanderers.

Through creative human engineering and progress, we've developed refrigerators to keep our food safe, vaccines to keep disease away, cars and planes to make travel easy on us, internet to make cross-continental communication instantaneous, and we're developing even more complex technologies that will make life easier and more comfortable for future generations.

However, we cannot become complacent like the Israelites became. After the Israelites seized Israel, they enjoyed peace until the kingdom collapsed. For our modern world, that collapse could come about from environmental destruction and negligence. When we forget that the world is precious and beloved by God, we do so unto our own detriment.

Humanity can't live without a world, and can't exist without physical space, at least in this life. Though we may never see effects of our actions in our lifetime, future generations certainly will. Even more so, many communities, especially ocean-front communities, that we never interact with have received the punishment for our overindulgence and environmental carelessness.

When waves of trash wash up on beaches in the Dominican Republic, the largest landfill in the world is two thousand two hundred acres, and Australia's Great Barrier Reef is devastated so severely by global warming that more than one third of the reef has died as of 2016, we can see that our actions are causing irreparable harm to the world we rely on and the world that God loves.

This new reality highlights how important it is that we weave love and respect for the environment back into Christianity. As strongly as Christians fight for their beliefs in other realms, Christianity is oddly silent or even regressive when it comes to championing the environment and protecting our God-given world. So, as Christians, we must renew our vigor and fight passionately to protect our world and give it the respect that we would give to anything that God, our Heavenly Father, loves.

WHY SHOULD THEY LISTEN?

For us as mentors, we may find that the environment is an oddly touchy subject. People have powerful reactions and political affiliations that color how they view the environment. For some, we ought not touch nature or if we do, we are evil in the sight of God. For others, nature is something for mankind to ignore, rule, or subjugate.

When we discuss the environment with people who might have knee jerk reactions to the topic, it is important that we keep the conversation biblically-centered. By showing that the environment is something that we ought to protect and also use for our benefit, according to scripture, we can help to sidestep people's long-held and deep-seated opinions that may color the discussion.

Taking a hard stance either way does not benefit our progress as humanity, nor does it benefit our sustainability. Instead, by showing that the Bible teaches that we are a part of the environment and beloved by God, we can mentor those around us to take their role as environmental stewards seriously.

When we highlight that environment is a critical part of the story of the Bible, from the Exodus to Jesus fasting in the wilderness, we can bring about environmental enlightenment that may have hitherto not taken place. It is important for us to participate in the environment, but also safeguard it. A scriptural argument can convey the gravity of our role in the environment in an appealing way to those that we mentor. By removing politics or personal beliefs from the conversation, we can highlight a moderate, guided approach to environmental use balanced by environmental conservation.

We also need to remind those we mentor that they are a part of the environment. When we ignore the dangers of how we get our energy or throw away our trash, we are harming our future selves. It is similar to leaving dishes to pile up until there is no room left in the kitchen. When we ignore the problem, it goes from something manageable to an insurmountable task.

SCRIPTURE AND THE ENVIRONMENT

To create compelling and clear scriptural arguments, it is important that we understand the scriptures and how setting in the scripture highlights the importance of environment. Biblical narratives are rarely devoid of place, and often God Himself uses environmental arguments to highlight His higher spiritual teachings.

For example, it would be difficult for us to understand Psalm twenty-three if we didn't have a concept of green pastures and quiet, clean waters. When our main mode of transportation is by car or plane, we fail to understand the necessity of God leading us down the right paths. There is nothing wrong with taking a plane or driving, but when those modes of transportation make us feel as though we are separate from the environment, we can fail to understand how important the environment is for our physical and spiritual health.

When we look at the life of Christ, some of His most profound spiritual moments were moments steeped in nature. Peter walking on the water is not possible if our lakes and rivers dry up. Christ going out into the wilderness to fast and pray is another moment where He finds God by entering into the isolation of nature. One of Christ's final moments before His capture by the Roman authorities was at the Garden of Gethsemane. Christ encounters God here to the point that He is sweating blood.

By understanding that Christ used nature as an avenue to encounter His Father, we can appreciate the value of nature and what it offers us as Christians. Highlighting this to our mentees and those who advocate for either extreme of environmental interaction helps us express how integral the environment is for our spiritual life.

Finally, recalling the glory of Eden and its status as a perfect world for man, we can understand that our technology, while not inherently evil, can cause us to lose sight of God. Everything in Eden perfectly provided for Adam and Eve, and they were charged with the work of caring for that garden. Because our world is fallen, it is even more important that we care for what we have. Our world cannot last forever, and it is important, out of love for those who will come after us, that we try to keep our world as clean and stable as possible.

When we ignore this imperative, we sin. By committing sins that extend beyond ourselves, we impact and damage the lives of neighbors we will never know. Even simple acts such as littering or wasting food has consequences that we cannot understand. In the words of Dostoyevsky in the Brothers' Karamazov, "Everyone is really responsible for all men and for everything." When we consider our actions as isolated events or against one person, we fail to understand how far reaching our actions can be.

A few littered bottles may seem inconsequential, but those bottles add up and last for thousands of years. So, it is important that in our mentoring and ethical advising that we highlight the importance of practical efforts in the lives of those we mentor. The life of a

Christian concerned about the environment is not just cerebral, but one of action. Simply picking up litter after someone, even if it isn't yours, goes a long way to pave the way for a healthier, cleaner environment.

One way that we can exercise this practically as church members and leaders is to organize clean-up days in our community. In this way, we become like the early church in Acts,[9] where the church provided for those in need and had one mind. They worked onto self-sacrifice for the benefit of the church, and there is no better way to show how much the church cares than by doing the work that no one else wants to do.

This same drive and compassion for others caused the early church to create the first hospitals, and we have a great opportunity now to lead the world in practical, environmental work. As children of God, redeemed by Christ's love, we ought to love what God loves and care for it, including the environment. We cannot have a pie-in-the-sky mentality, believing that the world does not matter because Christ will return, and we will receive a new earth. Instead, as Christians, it is our responsibility to imitate and foster the love that God has for His creation in ourselves and in others.

---

[9]   Acts 2:41-47

CHAPTER 11

The Truth About Racial and Ethnic Relations

It is impossible for the world to forget the tragedy and pain that slavery brought into the world. When we look at the suppressive role that slavery and subsequent legislation like Jim Crow Laws filled in America, we can begin to understand the plight that many black families have to overcome simply to get by.

This is most clearly highlighted in old money. Everyone knows of established, wealthy families and if we follow the history of their money back, oftentimes the roots of family money run deep. This holds true across the globe, from England to China. The opposite holds true as well. It can take a family up to fifteen generations to obtain established wealth and stability.[1] I had never seen this more clearly than after my church began our yearly Home Christmas Make over, where we bring gifts and food to families in need. Our idea was that this would be a great way to bless those in our community and minister to them. What we found was that our actions were doing quite the opposite and were putting those we were trying to bless in real danger.

I realized this when we were dropping off gifts at one of the homes. We had carefully chosen a brand-new basketball to give to a young boy, and due to the way it was wrapped, it was clear what it was. He picked up the package with his eyes alight, and a smile played across his face. He even tried to bounce it while it had

---

[1]   *Family wealth lasts for ten to fifteen generations,* New Republic, 2014

"When we fail to realize the ways that the past affects the present, we can be blind."

the wrapping paper on it. *Success*, I thought. I only thought it for a moment, until a frown creased across his older brother's face that made my stomach drop.

The older brother said, "You'd better put that ball down. It's gonna get you killed. You better pick up a gun."

My team was appalled. "Oh, young man, don't say that!"

But it hit me. I just put that boy at risk. If he goes outside with that basketball, he's a target. He could get jacked for that basketball, and that could mean getting shot.

We thought that we were bringing blessings into that house, but all we did was create a target. So, we switched our model to something different. We didn't understand, as people outside of that community, what we had done.

When we fail to realize the ways that the past affects the present, we can be blind. In this case, we had to change our approach to our Home Christmas Makeover because generational discrimination and unethical laws had formed a foundation of material lack that gripped that community. This caused that boy's family to live in fear of showing any signs of prosperity. When people live in this reality, they sometimes resort to other illegal and even life-threatening or life-ending ways to get what they don't have. People have been killed over something as mundane as a pair of sneakers or a few dollars.[2] People also can be overcome with a spirit of jealousy that causes them to react in unhealthy ways when they see others with certain material possessions.

While we cannot undo the things in the past that have helped to position some of our communities in this way, we *can* change the future, but part of that means that we have a responsibility to understand the community of those we mentor and lead. Without understanding and intentional relationship building, we do more harm than good. When it comes to race, it is important that we take the time to foster interracial relationships and not just with model members of other races. When it comes to cross-ethnic relations, it is important that we take the time to develop greater cultural awareness, and that others may have a weaker economic position and may not have been exposed to the same opportunities or experiences that we have.

By learning and experiencing more about how others live and struggle, why they are in the position they are in, and why they feel and think the way they do, we can come closer to not only understanding our cultural and socio-economic differences, but caring enough about them to want to be a part of a larger solution that brings about change. Only when we arrive at a place of understanding that turns into genuine caring

---

[2]   *Mother of slain teen says son was killed over $200 pair of Air Jordan sneakers,* Washington Post, 2017

"Only when we arrive at a place of understanding that turns into genuine caring and action can we hope to bring about healing in the space of racial and ethnic relations."

and action can we hope to bring about healing in the space of racial and ethnic relations.

When we think about how to do this, it is more than just saying, "love your neighbor" or "have interracial and interethnic relationships." We can learn practical ways of speaking out against oppression by looking at the ways that others in the past have responded to it. When we look to Nelson Mandela, we can see how strongly he pushed for the end of apartheid. Mandela pressed on for a peaceful solution by connecting himself with others.

Mandela did not end apartheid alone. He called out to other countries and communities in the south of Africa, and he also crossed cultural and geographical borders by calling on other foreign leaders, like Pope John Paul II, President George H. W. Bush, and UK Prime Minister Margaret Thatcher. In the same way, we need to leverage our connections with those more powerful than us and with those that we mentor, to create change through relationship.

"When we take the view that
a person is superior or inferior
based on their race, we have
succumbed to racist thinking."

TERMS AND CONDITIONS

Part of being able to properly navigate this topic is learning the terms that surround it. Many times, people use words like racism and discrimination interchangeably, and some people may even use terms like unconscious bias. Part of being able to mentor effectively is to understand what these words and phrases mean so that we can have an informed discussion on the topic.

Understanding the words that we use to discuss these topics will help us to better understand others and to better explain to others why certain behavior or ideas are morally wrong.

Racism is a term that has seen a bit of misuse in the current climate and media. Racism has to do with how a person thinks, even if it is in a positive way. For example, believing that an Asian person is going to be better at math or that a Latino is more likely to commit a crime is racist. When we take the view that a person is superior or inferior based on their race, we have succumbed to racist thinking.

Oftentimes this may be more implicit than we think. In this case, people can have an implicit bias against people, even of their own race. For example, a group of black students hanging out at a park may draw the attention of a police officer more readily than if the group was comprised of white students. This implicit bias may not even be a conscious choice but rather, may be born out of racist predispositions.

We can even apply this to topics outside of race and ethnicity. If you stop and think about it, you're probably more likely to give your attention to a person that you find attractive or you may think that Christians are kinder than atheists or that people in your chosen political party are more intelligent.

Unconscious bias is the most common way that racist ideas come out of a person. Usually their intent isn't to harm, but is, rather, informed by their subconscious ideas and preconceived notions. This sometimes leads to discrimination, where a person acts on their ideas. This is a bit different than when people use words that they might not understand have a racist background, like "hooligan," which was used to describe "dirty and drunk" Irishmen.

When a person hires more white candidates than black, Asian, or Latino candidates, even though the black, Asian or Latino candidates are just as qualified, they are discriminating. Discrimination has much more far reaching consequences than racism, even explicit racism. When people are put down or pushed out because someone is discriminating against them, they may lose opportunities that they shouldn't have.

When we see discrimination, our reaction should be condemnation, but when we see racist ideas leaking out into our conversations or relationships, our response should be compassion and healing. Discrimination is a terrible crime. Racism is a painful and offensive slap. Both are awful, but by being able to identify and correct racist ideas, we can prevent unconscious bias from turning into unconscious discrimination.

We can never hope to help those we mentor or relate to by name calling them as racist without stooping down to help them understand why. This can be a harrowing process, especially when the typical reaction to being called out is to deny, but it is something that we are called to do.

WHY SHOULD THEY LISTEN?

In many cases, no one wants to discuss race, ethnicity, racism, and discrimination directly, especially with members of other races, except maybe on social media. Opinions on racial and ethnic issues vary wildly. Asking an Asian person about affirmative action will likely net you a different response than if you asked a black or even a white person. Because opinions and emotions can range wildly about the topic of race, even between members of the same race, people tend to avoid the topic altogether.

Even worse, our news media and even political systems often pick up stories about race for a moment but fail to generate meaningful discussion on the matter. It is easier to highlight issues like police brutality and

"By having friends in low and high places and of different skin tones and worldviews, we increase our voice exponentially."

mass incarceration in the news cycle, which is more commonly directed at African Americans,[3] than to help organize an effort to create change.

However, by entering into relationships with those of other races and ethnicities, we can come to create important personal connections with them that can bring about understanding that will lead to action and compassion. Without relationship building, we can never hope to bring about an end to racism.

Moses understood the importance of relationship in his ministry to the Israelites. When the people had disputes, Moses would listen to the Israelites and make judgements. He was freely accessible to help his people. While this ultimately led to Moses burning out, Moses continued to hear important cases but also trained others to settle smaller disputes in his stead.

When we look at Moses' life, he was positioned to speak to Pharaoh because he was his adoptive grandson. By understanding and participating in Egyptian life,

---

[3]   *What the data really says about police and racial bias,* Vanity Fair, 2016

Moses was able to find an audience with Pharaoh that others would have never been able to receive.

Our reach and power are limited by those we surround ourselves with. When we limit ourselves to only mentoring and leading those of our own race or ethnicity, we will be ineffective when it comes to interacting with issues surrounding those very topics. By having friends in low and high places and of different skin tones and worldviews, we increase our voice exponentially.

When we are a symbol of peace and love to our community and outside of it, our voice gains echoes. Our friends will speak up for us when someone makes a racial or ethnic comment behind our backs. Our friends will spread the message that we are spreading. Eventually, the echoes will become a chain reaction, and we will no longer have to speak with our own voice, but among a cacophony of other voices. There is power numbers.

WHO SHOULD I TELL THEM SENT ME?

Racism has historically been justified using the Bible, especially when it came to slavery. Heresies, such as the mark of Cain, have created disturbing and violent ideologies that have formed scars in the minds and lives of many people. Even more, people have suggested that the Bible forbids interracial marriages and condones slavery itself.

Because of this, it can be difficult as Christians to speak fruitfully about race and ethnic relations. It can be difficult when churches are so visibly segregated, not only by race but nationality. This can be especially difficult when some self-professed Christians are vehemently racist.

Our task can seem almost unsurmountable, but by embodying Christ, we can make practical headway in healing the damage that has been done falsely in the name of Christ. By living a life that shows our love for our neighbor, be they of any race, we can help restore the image of Christianity in the minds of those we lead and mentor.

Consider what Paul said in his letter to the Galatians, "There is neither Jew nor Gentile, neither slave nor free, nor is there male and female, for you are all one in Christ Jesus."[4] Paul is not saying here that he doesn't see race, but instead makes it clear that Christ's mission was one of unity. That does not mean that we are not individuals, but it means that we do share Christ in common.

By making a point to first bridge the gaps that exist in the church, we can begin to form valuable relationships with our brothers and sisters in Christ. When we come together as Christians, we come with love and respect for our siblings in Christ. When we treat them with Christ-like patience and Christ-like acceptance, we can begin to reform the stereotypes and preconceived notions that we have about those of other races.

---

[4]   Galatians 3:28 NIV

Establishing these relationships within our churches keeps us from acting as hypocrites, asking for racial reconciliation, laws, and protections but not interacting or integrating with those around us and maintaining latent, subtle racist tendencies. Real relationship is the only cure to racism, and the best and safest place for us to bring about racial healing is within the church. If we can't learn to love, accept, and celebrate our brothers and sisters, certainly we can't expect or ask those outside the church to do so.

By having this base of relationship, we can, however, go to the world and offer them an example of the peace that we hope for. By living it, day in and day out, we can teach ourselves and others how to navigate the perilous space that is discussions about race. Be we black, white, Asian, Native American or something else, we can only enter this space by making real relationship.

God's message continually reinforces the importance of relationship with us. From God walking in the Garden of Eden to Christ taking on twelve friends as His disciples, the importance of relationship is a consistent theme. If we don't take this seriously, we have failed to recognize an important part of God's message of reconciliation to humanity.

WHY SHOULD THEY LISTEN?

The extension of grace and forgiveness to others is a value that God commands we take seriously. This does not mean that we let people use us as doormats, but it does mean that we make sincere efforts to mend relationships. We must emulate Christ's long-suffering and persistence when we mentor and teach others about racism. God did not choose David because of his appearance or age. He was the youngest and smallest of Jesse's children. And, Christ did not give up on the men who were crucifying Him either, crying out to God saying, "Father, forgive them, for they know not what they do."[5]

By taking Christ's attitude seriously, we can become agents of healing and reconciliation. If we act with hatred or vitriol, as deserved as we may think it is, we simply push people further away from us. By being compassionate and merciful, just like our God, we can bring about change. Had Christ said, "Come to me, all those who are perfect and make no mistakes," heaven would be empty. In the same way, if we say to those who make mistakes or hurt us, especially when it comes to race, that we don't want them in our lives, we will find that our lives become ineffective. We will never be able to help others make the changes that they need to make in their behavior or thinking. But when we have proven ourselves to love unto hurting, we can open up the hearts of others and bring about healing.

Near the end of her life, a holocaust survivor and Christian, Corrie Ten Boom, gave a speech on forgiveness. She tells a story about when she encountered a guard of the concentration camp that

---

[5]   Luke 23:24 KJV

she was in, who she called one of the cruelest. The guard came up to her when she was giving a talk after the war in Berlin and said, "Ms. Ten Boom, don't you remember me?"

She recognized him immediately, and he told her that he had now become a Christian, and he asked if she could forgive what he did.

She admits that she could not. She remembered how her sister died in that concentration camp, and she remembered her suffering and how he had caused it. But she remembered the verse that comes after the Lord's Prayer, "But if you do not forgive others their sins, your Father will not forgive your sins."[6]

She knew that she could not forgive him alone, but she knew that God's love was stronger than her hatred. And through the strength of the Holy Spirit, she found the ability to forgive that guard. She shook his hand and forgave him.

Corrie Ten Boom's story is an extreme example of forgiveness. She knew that she couldn't forgive that cruel concentration camp guard, but she knew that God could. She found the strength to do so through God's power.

The cruel guard also had to ask for forgiveness. It likely took mentoring, time, and grace for the man to not only understand that he needed to ask for forgiveness, but also to generate the courage to ask for it. Someone had to sit with that man, tell him about God's grace, and

---

[6]   Matthew 6:15 NIV

"When we can forgive those who hurt us and ask forgiveness from those we have hurt, we can encounter the true love of Christ, and only then can we facilitate effective mentorship and relationship."

tolerate him enough to love him enough to share the Gospel with him. Through that process, healing took place, not just for the guard and his relationship with God, but also between the guard and Ms. Ten Boom.

It's unlikely that most of us have suffered the way that someone who lived through a concentration camp did, and it is important that we understand the importance of forgiveness in not only our lives but the lives of those who cross us. When we can forgive those who hurt us and ask forgiveness from those we have hurt, we can encounter the true love of Christ, and only then can we facilitate effective mentorship and relationship.

PRACTICAL RELATIONSHIP

It is one thing to campaign for equal rights and vote to support it. It is another thing to live a life of integration and healing. Paying lip service is not enough in today's world. No matter how much we try to regulate race via laws, we will never see racism die unless relationship heals those wounds.

It is important that we mentor and lead those around us to actively engage in relationships that span cultures, races, and socio-economic status. In the context of relationship, we can call out racist ideas that we see, and we can help guide those we mentor towards Christ-like thinking. Without these relationships, though, even our help might turn to hurt. Hurt comes along easily when we attempt to help without understanding the situation.

If you know nothing about automobiles and try to work on your friend's car, you may do more harm than good when you put anti-freeze in their oil pan. In the same way, we might give someone that we're trying to help a basketball that ends up putting them in danger.

We can help only after we've built up relationships. If we try to help those in need, help end racism, or help bridge cultural divides without these relationships, we're going to cause more pain. These relationships teach us important lessons and give us invaluable insight. When we've gained this, we can help educate and guide those legal policies, but without an interracial and intercultural approach, we can never hope to do anything valuable, let alone bring about the reconciliation that we desperately need.

CONCLUSION
The Practical, Modern Mentor

Today, people have a difficult time connecting with others. Advances in telecommunications has encouraged dependence on text messages, fast food has replaced family meal times, and many of us rely on the Internet to attend school, shop, chat, date, and share life experiences. The overall proliferation of social media has shifted how we communicate and connect with people.

To be an effective, modern mentor, we must be able to help others navigate the current age that we are living in, with all of it's new and emerging challenges. When we are faced with new data and claims, we ought to take them seriously and investigate diligently so that we can provide help to those in need. But even more than that, we need to remember that we are helping real human beings. We cannot let our modern world blot out the humanity of others.

One of the greatest privileges that we have as mentors in this age is that we can mentor in a way that is relational and healing. By engaging those we mentor on a personal level, we can help to dispel and abate the damages that some of our modern technologies have caused.

"Often, when we think of ourselves as leaders or mentors, we think of our students as eager and hungry to learn."

To do this, we have to create active mentorship that is not simply an impartation of ideas, but a planned relationship with those we mentor and an open attitude to whom we mentor.

A WELCOMING LIFE

In Luke 15, the "tax collectors and sinners" gather around to hear Jesus. However, the Pharisees and teachers of the law scoffed at Him. The whole of the chapter focuses on themes of finding, reclaiming, and accepting what has been lost, and the highest priority of the Kingdom of God is finding lost souls.

Even today, the stewards of the religious practice can sometimes be judgmentally critical, particularly of the kinds of people that Jesus embraced and fellowshipped with. The Pharisees did not view those who were sinners to be fit for the kingdom of God. Of course, that begs the question "Who could possibly get in?" Ultimately, the Pharisees believed that only the people they deemed worthy were fit for the kingdom of God, and anyone unlike them was disqualified.

In our modern world, this idea persists. Often, when we think of ourselves as leaders or mentors, we think of our students as eager and hungry to learn. But those who Christ had gathered around Him were the last people that we would think of as ready to accept His teachings, let alone ours.

The Pharisees viewed Jesus' crowd as less than desirable and unworthy of the kingdom of God, and in their eyes, Jesus was guilty of welcoming sinners into His life. And He was guilty. Despite these sinners having been denied access to the synagogue, Jesus invited them to sit with Him and eat with Him. By eating with and welcoming sinners, Jesus exposed the sin of the Pharisees' hospitality.

Throughout the Gospel, Jesus teaches us the importance of having a welcoming spirit. In each of our interpersonal encounters, we must lay out a welcoming spirit as if we were placing an offering on the altar of our hearts. Then, those we interact with can experience through us how the Lord is welcoming them, regardless of their condition.

By welcoming others into our life, we can embrace them. With this style of interpersonal interaction, we are making a small reflection of Christ's sacrifice on the cross. We are showing them the self-denial, self-sacrifice and warm embrace that was Christ's life, death, and resurrection.

Jesus celebrated His connection with sinners, and this is precisely how we ought to relate with one another. By living a welcoming life, we do more than tolerate others and survive encounters. Instead, we gladly accept those who God has placed in our lives, and in that way, we serve God. By doing this, we help to

> "By welcoming others into our life, we can embrace them. With this style of interpersonal interaction, we are making a small reflection of Christ's sacrifice on the cross."

recreate the world that we live in and show those that we mentor that they are an important part of the fabric of our society.

We can never hope to be effective mentors, especially in a world that is becoming more and more depersonalized, without living this way of life. We may be able to teach model students how to live a God-honoring life, but we will never be able to show them. We will simply create more Pharisees. Our lives ought to show, not simply tell those we mentor how to live. But if we cannot personally embrace the unwanted or the sinner, we can never hope to facilitate the change that we want to see in the world, even at the smallest level.

If all of our friends are holy and righteous, we need a more diverse cast of friends. If those we mentor are only people that we would want to be friends with, we're closing our eyes to those who need our mentorship the most.

"Mentors must constantly be pushing themselves further and further when it comes to their knowledge and their practice."

LIVING MENTORSHIP

Being an effective mentor is not a glamorous role. Mentors must constantly be pushing themselves further and further when it comes to their knowledge and their practice. A mentor who knows everything but cannot express it with love and patience is nothing.[1] In the same vein, a mentor who only mentors perfect students is playing pretend. Perfect students are going to learn with or without a teacher, but if we leave the imperfect students behind because they are too much effort, we're failing to be like Christ.

It is important that we teach those who we mentor to sit and eat with those that they might find undesirable, just like Christ did. When we bring these people into our lives, it doesn't mean that it will be easy, but our relationships with these people ought to be so influential that they decide they want to meet the God who has given us life and wisdom.

A part of this mentoring life is to use our technology to connect in positive ways with those we mentor. By

---

[1]   1 Corinthians 13:12

"When we mentor, we are creating new disciples and teaching them about what Christ has done and how He wants us to live."

---

dropping a message or video-chatting someone, we can help reinforce that they are a valuable person, especially when many of the other messages or images they see may suggest otherwise.

Without living out our mentoring, we can never hope to be effective mentors to others. If all we do is create new Pharisees and rich young rulers, we can never hope to inspire our mentees to care about those in the LGBT community, about race, about the environment, or any other topic that doesn't directly concern them.

In Matthew 28, Jesus delivers the Great Commission to His disciples. The idea of discipleship is akin to the idea of mentorship. When we mentor, we are creating new disciples and teaching them about what Christ has done and how He wants us to live. But it isn't enough to simply impart knowledge. Our mentorship and discipleship must be a lived experience.

As ethical mentors we should always be loving and compassionate, but we should also never forget that God wants us to seek ways to change, ask for forgiveness, become the best that we can be, and to work diligently at overcoming our struggles. We must always work to align our will with God's and find ways to teach others how to do this. With God and His Word as our foundation, we can show people Christ's example and guide them towards true life. Instead of conforming God to our will, we have to participate in self-sacrifice and say, "Not my will but yours be done."[2]

Finally, we must cultivate a life that shows everyone we mentor that, no matter their past or current circumstance, they can meet Christ face to face and that He desires to enter into a genuine loving relationship with them. Do not be afraid to stand firm in your faith and ready to stand for what is good and right in God's eyes, but do so with the greatest compassion and sincere will to understand how we are different and why we are different. Only then can we position ourselves to exhibit the true character of Christ and bring meaningful change to our world.

---

[2]   Luke 22:42 NIV

BIOGRAPHY

At the age of 17, Dr. William H. Curtis accepted the call to ministry. He currently serves as Senior Pastor of the Mount Ararat Baptist Church, a large, urban ministry that ministers to more than 10,000 members in the community. In addition, Dr. Curtis has been an instructor at the United Theological Seminary, and is Co-Owner of The Church Online, LLC, a successful full-service marketing, technology, and publishing company.

Dr. Curtis holds a Bachelor of Arts Degree in Religious Studies and Philosophy from Morgan State University, a Master of Divinity Degree from Howard University School of Divinity, and a Doctor of Ministry Degree from United Theological Seminary in Dayton, Ohio.

He is the author of two other popular books, *Dressed for Victory: Putting on the Full Armor of God* and *Faith: Learning to Live Without Fear*.

Dr. Curtis is married to Mrs. Christine Curtis, and they are the proud parents of one lovely daughter, Houston.